The Quest for Maleness

THÉUN MARES

NOTE FROM THE AUTHOR

Those readers who are intending to read this book as well as *Unveil the Mysteries of the Female*, should take note that the contents in many parts of these two books are more or less identical. This is necessarily so because of the nature of the material covered. Nonetheless, the wise reader will not be tempted to skip reading an apparent repeat, for although the content can be the same, the approach is nonetheless very different, and throws much light upon the more subtle differences between male and female.

OTHER BOOKS BY THÉUN MARES

The Toltec Teachings Series:
Return of the Warriors
Cry of the Eagle
The Mists of Dragon Lore

This Darned Elusive Happiness
Unveil the Mysteries of the Female

What people have been saying about Theun's work ...
"Required reading for anyone serious about really living life."
"I love his sense of humour and adaptability to everyday life situations."
"These books changed my life."
"I bought your book about four weeks ago now... what resulted was a "magical journey," which continues today."

THE Quest FOR Maleness

THÉUN MARES

Lionheart
PUBLISHING

To Neil, my successor, with whom I share a bond that can be shared only between two of our kind; to Charles, the most cheerfully co-operative editor and publisher I could possibly have wished for; to Christiaan, a deeply sensitive being that can be as playful as a puppy; to James, a private man of few words who is always there when needed most; to Geoffrey, for whom every challenge is a new adventure; to Russell, whose quiet strength and deep warmth have brought me to love him like a son; and to Oso, who brings a meaning to friendship that cannot be expressed in words. To have these males accompany me on this quest for maleness is a special privilege, and to observe each of them uncovering their potential, each in their own unique way, is a moving experience that adds a great richness and fullness to my own life.

© Théun Mares 1999

All rights reserved. No part of this book may be reproduced by any means or in any form whatsoever, without written permission from the publisher, except for brief quotations embodied in literary articles or reviews.

ISBN 1-919792-07-4

Cover illustration by Gavin Calf
DTP design by Mandy McKay
Printed and bound by Cape & Transvaal Book Printers, Parow, Cape.

Lionheart
PUBLISHING

Private Bag X5, Constantia 7848, Cape Town, South Africa
Phone: +27 21 794-4923
FAX: +27 21 794-1487
e-mail: lionheart@toltec-foundation.org
www.toltec-foundation.org
www.elusivehappiness.com

ABOUT THE AUTHOR

THE AUTHOR WAS BORN in Zimbabwe, of a mother who was a natural seer, and a father who was a miner. Having a seer's ability himself, Théun was trained from an early age in this art and in the disciplines of the Toltec tradition. Toltec means "A man or woman of knowledge," and the Toltec tradition encompasses a vast and ever-expanding system of knowledge about life, the universe and the part that we play within both.

Drawing upon his knowledge of the fundamental unity of all of life, the author has used his seer's skills and training to uncover the essential truths that lie at the heart of all true religions and belief systems. In his books, he reveals the nature of these core truths, which have so often become distorted, corrupted and lost with the passage of time. He also shows how we can use these truths in a practical manner to revolutionize our thinking, our behaviour and our world.

The author's career has spanned the breadth of the performing arts, education and business. He now lives in Cape Town with Marianne, where he divides his time between writing, teaching and creating courses for adults and teenagers.

The overall aim of Théun's work is firstly, to rekindle in all of us the knowledge that the whole purpose of life is the evolution of awareness, and secondly, to imbue in us an understanding of how this is best achieved.

His message is that the only possible way for us to create a hope-filled future, rather than a world filled with destruction, is by developing the openness of heart to embrace all of life fully, rather than by becoming separative, divisive and by indulging in escapisms.

Embracing all of life involves meeting all our challenges head-on, rather than running away from them. It involves developing and maintaining respect for the world in which we live, and for life in general; it involves acknowledging that all our actions have an impact on those around us, and it also involves the constant willingness to respond – to take action – based upon the feedback we are getting from our lives. Introversion only implies cutting ourselves off from life.

The overall import of Théun's message is that, in the final analysis, the proper evolution of awareness can only come about as a result of practical experience. Wasting time in philosophizing, intellectualizing, rationalizing and escapisms only serve to lead one further and further away from practical experience, and from the real business of living. For the only thing of lasting value in life upon the physical plane is to live it all, to experience it all, to embrace it all: the good with the bad, and so to develop the sense of utter inclusiveness, which is the mark of a passionate, alive, and truly human, being with a heart.

TABLE OF CONTENTS

Preface		8
Introduction		11

Part One – The Mystery of Gender
1	Entering the world of the male	16
2	Getting to grips with your potential	23
3	The origin of gender	27
4	The dual nature of the female	40
5	Separating myth from reality	43

Part Two – The 9 Myths and their Hidden Keys
6	Myth One – Men don't cry	48
7	Myth Two – Men are aggressive	70
8	Myth Three – Men must be educated	80
9	Myth Four – Men must think	89
10	Myth Five – Men smoke and drink	98
11	Myth Six – Men are strong	113
12	Myth Seven – Men must be successful	129
13	Myth Eight – Men should be married	140
14	Myth Nine – Men are sexual studs	148

Part Three – Getting to know yourself as a Male
15	Role models	172
16	The over-dominant mother	176
17	The weak father	183
18	Hunting for power	188
19	The male perspective on relationships	199
20	The male pledge	211
21	Competition	221
22	The journey ahead	226

PREFACE

IF SOMEBODY ASKED YOU what it meant to be a male could you answer them? A few years ago I would not have been able to answer this with any clarity, except to say that being a male in modern times is not easy and that there are probably as many definitions of maleness as there are men. So how does one know if one is getting it right?

Across the world this question seems to be becoming more and more important for men. Everywhere there are men's groups springing up where men meet to enjoy the company and camaraderie of other men. But does playing drums or singing around campfires make you a true male?

When I was a boy I looked around the world and became so disillusioned with the actions of men that I was embarrassed at being associated with them. The most common display of "maleness" that I saw was a strange kind of bravado that seemed to have no real substance. Everywhere men seemed to be destructive and insensitive to the world. In school locker rooms boys joked crudely about females. Later they worked for large companies that were equally insensitive to the environmental impact of their work, or else they took office jobs that were so heartless that they seemed to completely wither away.

Thoughout my early years I had a string of male heroes. These were men who in some way seemed able to sense something more in life, men who had not lost their sense of adventure. I would watch their eyes gleam as they animatedly discussed their dreams for the world. But the sad truth is that few of these men have ever materialized any of their dreams.

How is it that the world could become so difficult, or men so weak and impractical, that most of the noblest ideas are never brought to fruition? What is the world coming to when even the heroes are giving up?

Through the work I have done as a student of Théun, I have learned that in order to turn the tide it is not necessary to save a nation or to lead a country into war. It is the little things in every individual's life that count the most – the little drops that eventually cause the bucket to overflow and start a ripple effect in the world. You and I *can* make a difference. If each man were to start to stand up and reclaim the honour, beauty and power of their true masculine potential, then the world would change. If you reclaim this power for yourself you will see the changes in the world around you.

How can one do this? That's what this book is all about. In the simple, practical language and style that is the hallmark of Théun's work he answers the question of what it is to be a male. Working from the premise that we have everything we need right here and now, Théun shows how, within the heart of commonly-held myths about maleness, lie the seeds of truth. He demonstrates how you can find this potential in your everyday life and how to encourage it to grow. True growth is never easy, but it is also far from impossible.

Working with the material contained in this book I have acquired a completely new experience of male awareness. I have seen the inspiration, beauty, hope and openness; the warmth and strength.

May you too have the courage to tackle this journey and may you also find as much joy in your journey as I have in mine.

Neil Mason-Jones

INTRODUCTION

*(Written for the male course held at
Hopefield on the weekend of 28-30th.May,1999)*

WHEN I LOOK AROUND in the world today, it is with a deep sense of anguish that I still hear echoing in my ears the haunting words of a female friend who asked, "Where have all the heroes gone?"

Yes! Indeed! What has happened to them all? No longer do men stand tall and proud in their masculinity. No longer are there bards who sing the honour of hero-saviours. The bards are gone because the hero-saviours are gone, and the ballads too are gone because the honour which men once carried with pride is also gone. But the deepest anguish of all comes from knowing that when the last of the bards died, so too did beauty. And when the last of the hero-saviours died, so too did hope. Without beauty and without hope, what is left? Nothing! Only a cold sterile world of crime and violence, of ugliness, injustice and despair, and a sickening sense of hopelessness that breeds a debilitating apathy.

Are there then, no heroes left? Are there no men left on this earth who can step forward to save the world from the greatest catastrophe that has ever befallen the human race? Are all men today so completely emasculated that they have become nothing more than semen donors, with some doing drugs in a futile effort to numb their minds and feelings to the pain of that emasculation? Are there no men left who are at least willing to try?

I know of no heroes still walking this earth, and I know of no saviours either. But I guess, in considering everything, that if I do not like what I see, then there is still me. Although I do not feel like much of a hero, I nevertheless am willing to try. And although I do not know too much about being a saviour, I am willing to learn.

But I realise that I do not know where to go, and from whom I will be able to learn what it is to be a hero-saviour. Yet I also know that if I do not know where to go, then "here" must be as good a place as any other; and if I do not know when I will find my way, then "now" must be the right time; and if I do not know from whom to learn, then I must teach myself.

So, what do I have that I can offer you right now, right here? In the greater scheme of things, I guess not much. In fact, perhaps not much at all! But I am willing to share with you as much as I can of the things I have learned upon my own quest for maleness. If, through my sharing, I am able to inspire in you a sense of what it is to be a true male, then that shall be my reward. If I can instil in you at least some sense of the beauty I have encountered upon my journey, then that shall be my joy. If I can impress upon you even just a little of the hope I have discovered along the way, then that shall be my honour. And if I can share with you my belief in the spirit of man, then

I shall look upon that as having been the real purpose of this weekend.

But, gentlemen, I do not wish you to labour under a false impression! It is not fanfares, white stallions, billowing capes and swords I am pursuing. Instead I am in search of the impeccable honour, the quiet dignity, the unwavering hope and the tenacious courage that is implied within the essence of the true male. If I can share with you some of this, by sharing my knowledge with you, then within my heart of hearts I shall know that I am a true male, a hero, and a saviour, for you must understand that any man is only as good as other men make him! For example, an army general may lead his troops into battle, but unless his men respect him enough to follow him, he rides alone to his death, in his heart a hero, yes, but in the eyes of his troops and his enemy, a lonely fool!

If it is a leader you are wanting, then I am willing to show you the way. But if what I tell you here does not call forth your respect, then I guess, come Monday morning, I will be riding on alone. In relation to this, know that although I too long for that uplifting camaraderie that exists between males who share a quest, I have long ago come to the conclusion that loneliness upon the quest is preferable to remaining in a world that has become filled with ugliness and despair, and that death is strangely more enticing than a life of hopelessness and apathy.

Therefore, and in honour of your wish, my friends, let us pause in this place for a brief while, and I will share with you what I have learned upon this quest. But know that no sunrise finds the male where sunset left him. After this sharing I will continue upon my quest, with or without you! In my heart of hearts I know what I seek. If you join me, I shall be en-joyed by your presence. If I go alone, then I will go alone!

This is the last male course I will teach. I have made this decision in honour of the human spirit. You see, gentlemen, I believe that you and every other man out there is ready and capable of finding your way and of claiming your power as a true male. But if I continue to teach this course, I will be implying that men in general, including you, are not yet ready, and therefore that you still need to be taught. However, I believe that you are ready, and that you can do it on your own! And to prove my belief in you, I am making this the final male course. This belief is my commitment to you, and to all other men.

PART ONE

THE MYSTERY OF GENDER

CHAPTER 1

ENTERING THE WORLD OF THE MALE

*Men and women have discarded the
obvious in favour of intellectual complexity,
and, as a result, have lost touch with their
feelings, including those feelings that
pertain to the mystery of gender.*

NO ONE CAN TELL YOU how to become a male, for the reason that every male is a unique individual. Other men can tell you what being male means to them, but how is that going to help you when you are not them? Women can tell you what they think men should be, but being women, they can no more teach you to be a male than a fish can teach a bird to fly! No! If you are going to enter the world of the true male, then you must first learn what that world is, and then you must learn how to claim it, how to make it your own.

This may sound like a complicated riddle, but actually it is simplicity itself! The trick lies in coming to the realisation that you do not have to go anywhere in search of anything, simply because you are already there, wherever "there" may be, and you already have everything you need, whatever "everything" may mean to you. What I am saying is that the quest for maleness is not a physical journey we undertake in search of something that is "out there." Instead it is a most magical journey that takes us into the deep space of our own inner being, to discover there the outer fringes of, what I term, *the void*.

Just to approach the fringes of that void is the most frightening experience I know of, for at first sight it appears as though entering the seemingly alien depths of those fringes would be like stepping into a bottomless abyss! But the fringes of the void are not an abyss, and neither are they bottomless. In fact, once you have got over the fright of stepping into them, they are every bit as solid as the physical world. It is only beyond the fringes that the true void lies, and when it is experienced from within the depths of its fringes, that void is the most spectacular sight to behold!

I purposely use the term "behold," for I do not know how else to express this exhilarating experience of utter magic! I cannot say "see," because how does one see unmitigated darkness? I cannot say "feel," for how does one feel a space that is empty? I cannot say "hear," for how does one hear a void? I also cannot say "taste" or "smell," because even these two senses are meaningless within the presence of the void. And yet, in a strange and inexplicable manner, something deep down inside slowly begins to register that somehow, perception of that void is only possible because something in one's innermost being is gripping it, or "holding" it in some odd way! It is because of this "gripping," this "holding onto," that I say "behold!"

What is this void? It is quite simply, no-thing! But this does not mean that I am speaking figuratively, or in symbols, or riddles, or metaphors. To behold the void is to know beyond any shadow of a doubt that it is more real than what is normally perceived as reality. To behold the void is to know that it is the very core of man's existence. But apart from the awesome sense of power that seems to radiate from out of its depths, how does one describe no-thing? How does one even begin to put words to *that* which leaves one speechless? All I can really tell you about the void, is that *It Is*. And because It Is, the core, every man deep down inside knows that It calls him, beckons him to enter its fringes and draw from it the full meaning of masculinity. Sadly though, because of its truly frightening nature, men nowadays choose not to acknowledge the sound of that call, and instead try to cover their ears with the clamour of a mundane existence.

More than that I am at a loss to explain. But what I can do, is to tell you about the incredible effects of accessing that void. But before I do this, in order for you to become aware of these effects you must first know that from a certain perspective, the terms "male" and "female", pertain to specific states of awareness. So, in order to grasp the meaning of the void, you must first grasp the secret of gender as it relates to awareness. That is the key to the void! Without that key you will never grasp the meaning of the void, much less be able to access it!

Realise that any awareness we may have, is something we bring about within ourselves. This last point is particularly important when it comes to considering our sexual identity. Because you were born a man, you have a specific gender, rather than being an "it." In practical terms this makes of you the opposite polarity to women, and not some sort of asexual oddity that falls somewhere in-between the two poles.

So, from a very basic level, there is your body, which is that of a man, and there is the you who indwells that body, possessing an awareness which is built up around your physical gender. Your awareness is of course not limited or, at least, it shouldn't be, for you can obviously develop your awareness to any level you choose, and in any direction you choose. The possible development of your awareness is what, for the purposes of this book, we will define as being your potential.

In relation to potential it is worthwhile to know that it comes from the root "potent," meaning quite literally your *ability*, or your *power*. So in talking about potential, we are talking about your inner hidden abilities and power which even you may not be aware of, or which perhaps you have never explored. Thus, for the sake of clarity, and not for the sake of prejudice, as some illiterates are given to believing, we define the potential in men as *masculinity*, and the potential in women as *femininity*.

THE WORLD OF THE MALE

= A STATE OF AWARENESS
which you must learn how
to claim and make YOUR OWN

Man = Gender = Your own physical body
Male = Your awareness
Masculinity = Your potential

Masculinity has its origin within the void, whilst femininity has its origin within the womb. Yet, in a strange kind of a way the void and the womb complement each other, in that the one is hidden within the innermost depths of the male psyche, and the other is concealed within the physical body of the female. Furthermore, the void has an immense power that radiates upward and outward, giving one the impression that it is not really an abyss, but some huge vortex that pulsates with an inner power pushing upward and outward. On the other hand, the womb is still, but brooding, forever ready to receive and to gather. The void is therefore constantly active, whilst the womb, until conception has taken place, is mostly passive. But all of this will become clearer as we progress in our consideration of masculinity.

So, to state the obvious, you are a being indwelling a body which has the physical gender termed *man*, you have an awareness termed *male*, and you have a potential which is termed *masculinity*, and which has its origin within the void. Now from this it should be quite clear that to want to develop any potential other than your own, would be to deny yourself your own inherent potential, and what good would that do you? Yet it is crazy to see how many men are trying to become females, and how many women are trying to become males, all in the name of sexual equality. If we were meant to be unisexual, then surely we would have been born hermaphrodites! It just doesn't make sense that men and women are trying to become an "it" when they have a potential that is clearly masculine or feminine. It is insanity that men today should be in search of the womb, rather than the void, and that women should have abandoned the womb in search of the void!

The purpose of this book is to give you some working tools which will put you in touch with your own feelings concerning masculinity, and to impart to you certain information that will enable you to use those feelings to help unfold your potential as a male. But more than this I cannot do, and neither can anyone else for that matter, irrespective of what claims or promises they may make. No-one can give you an awareness of what it is to be male – all of us have to claim our knowledge for ourselves and by ourselves. But there are nonetheless specific tools and select information that can be invaluable for assisting you to explore your feelings, and thereby to help you discover what the true nature of the world of the male is, and how you can make it your own.

Life is not an intellectual process –
life is a feeling.

If you find that you have glossed over the aphorism above, then pause to consider what an intellectual fool you are! Are you such a boring stereotype of the modern man that you have to intellectualise before you can think of how to achieve a physical erection? If you are, then is it surprising that you are so impotent in your life? Any act that is initiated by a feeling is a true creation, and any creation, irrespective of whether it is a musical composition, a new invention, an architectural marvel, an engineering miracle, or quite simply a baby, is an act requiring the only energy we have, namely, the sexual energy. So, if you can only get lead into your pencil by having to intellectualise, then you are not only out of touch with your feelings, but you are also to all intents and purposes impotent!

Many a man can testify to just how unfulfilling the sexual act can be on a boring Sunday afternoon. Even though it seemed like a good idea at the time, such a man finds it difficult to maintain his erection and, being bored out of his mind, it takes him forever to reach a climax. All in all, this is just like the lives of so many men today. The careers they follow seemed to be a good idea at the time, but why does that career need constant effort to keep it up? Their relationships or marriages also seemed to be a good idea, but why do those relationships or marriages never seem to reach the climax the men had longed for?

CHAPTER TWO

GETTING TO GRIPS WITH YOUR POTENTIAL

In dealing with mystery it is wise to bear in mind that one is up against the unknown. Only fools are so ignorant as to want to fake cleverness in the face of the unknown. The wise ones are sufficiently humble to allow their feelings to guide them.

LET ME BEGIN this chapter by stating that the scope of this book does not allow us to become too involved in technicalities that are enough to stretch even the ablest of minds to their limits. Yet, if we are to come to grips with your potential, which is inextricably tied up with the mystery of beingness, we cannot avoid acquiring at least a rudimentary understanding of that baffling secret we term the evolution of awareness. Therefore, although I will endeavour to keep everything as simple as possible in this book, if you would like a deeper insight into this particular section of the teachings, my first series of books will throw considerable light upon a subject which we are here going to gloss over very, very superficially.

Now, before we can look at what it means to be a male, we need to go back to another point which is so obvious that most people simply ignore it. In fact we have already touched upon this point, namely, that all of us are basically spirit beings indwelling a physical body. For the purposes of this book I am going to use the terminology of my own particular training, although, of course, you can use whatever terminology makes sense to you. What I am going to try to do is simply to sketch out for both of us a common meeting ground so that we will understand each other.

From my perspective, which is similar to that of most of the great world religions, man is primarily a spirit being who comes into incarnation. Now whether you wish to believe that this happens only once, or whether you wish to believe in re-incarnation, doesn't actually matter. Whatever you choose to believe, one way or another the spirit being, that is, you, comes into incarnation. However, it is not that the spirit being itself comes into incarnation, but rather that its *awareness* comes to indwell a physical body on the physical plane. Toltecs term this incarnating awareness *the dreamer*, but we do not need to get hung up on terminology. If you prefer, you can term this the soul, or the reincarnating ego, or the higher self, or whatever else you like, as long as you understand what I mean by *the dreamer*. Remember that it is essentially the *awareness* of a being we are referring to at this point.

THE MYSTERY OF GENDER

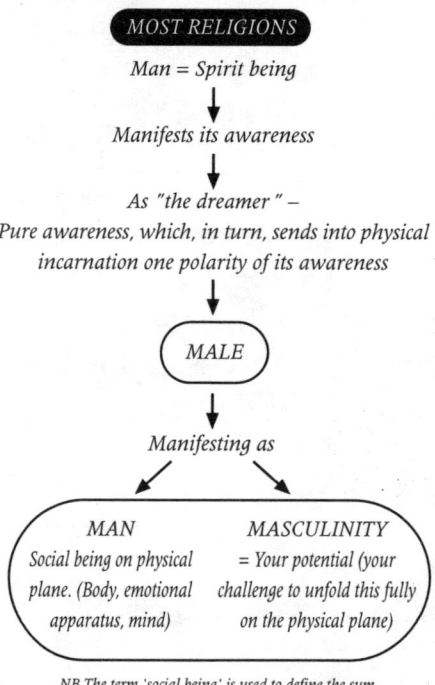

NB The term 'social being' is used to define the sum total of physical body, emotional apparatus, and the mind

What you should always keep in mind regarding this awareness, i.e., the dreamer, is that the term "male" refers to the one polarity of its existence, and that the term "female" refers to its other polarity. This means that whenever we speak about male, we are referring to a specific polarity of the dreamer's awareness, and not to the male body as such. Your physical body is simply an expression of your masculine potential, and it is this physical expression which we term "man." Clearly, what this implies is that you, the spirit being, have already incarnated one polarity of your awareness upon the physical plane by taking upon yourself a physical body termed "man." Further, that one polarity of your awareness is not just what we term "male," since it also has a potential which is masculine by nature. From all this it stands to reason that the whole purpose of incarnating is to unfold or to develop your potential, or, in other words, to unfold your full awareness of what it is to be male.

This is the same thing as saying that to be a true male implies that you are manifesting your full potential, which is masculine, upon the physical plane, as a man. If this sounds overly obvious, as it should, then have a good look around you. Out of all the thousands of men you can see, how many would you term true males? Would you call yourself a true male?

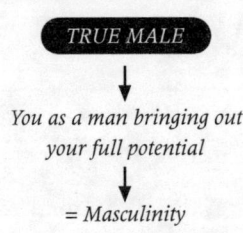

CHAPTER THREE

THE ORIGIN OF GENDER

*Locked within the secret of gender lie the
keys to evolution. The man or woman who has
mastered the secret of gender has unlimited
power at his or her command.*

IN THE PREVIOUS CHAPTER we saw that the terms "male" and "female" refer to the two polarities of our awareness, and that through the act of incarnation we manifest either of these two polarities in terms of manhood or womanhood. The implication of all this is, naturally, that every man has an inner female counterpart, and that every woman has an inner male counterpart, since these are the two polarities of our awareness.

With respect to the nature of these two polarities, the male represents the spirit of man, and the female represents the physical being, that is, the incarnation, of man. (By the term "man" I am referring to those spirit beings broadly referred to as mankind). Toltecs term these two polarities the *nagal* (pronounced na-hal) and the *tonal* respectively, and it is through the interaction between these two polarities that the evolution of awareness takes place. Therefore we have:

$$\text{MALE} = \text{NAGAL (the spirit of man)}$$
$$\text{FEMALE} = \text{TONAL (the physical being)}$$

In case you are already thinking that this smacks too much of sexual inequality, let me explain a little more. First, remember that we are all spirit beings in physical incarnation and, as a result, all of us, irrespective of gender, have a nagal and a tonal. Second, remember also that in speaking of male and female we are referring to states of awareness, and that all awareness is relative to other states of awareness, irrespective of whether the actual physical manifestation of that awareness is masculine or feminine in gender. In *This Darned Elusive Happiness* I explained the relative factor of awareness, but for our present understanding we now need to look a little more deeply at what this actually implies. To do so, let us consider the grand scheme of things.

If we look at life in its totality, we keep coming back to that age-old question: "What am I?" Although we have already answered this question, we still do not really know what our answer means. Clearly, this is a type of question we can answer only partially, in that all we can safely say about ourselves is what we know ourselves to be in physical terms. Therefore rather than try to answer a question that lies beyond our present capability of answering, let us rather ask the question in such a way that we can answer it, if only in part. Thus the real question is: "What is this *me* termed the tonal?" or: "What is this *me* termed the physical being?"

This *me* which is the physical being, the tonal, has, as we all know, a physical body which is not only capable of sensory perception, but through which it is also possible to perceive in terms of emotional responses, as well as mental impulses. This is the physical plane manifestation of ourselves. But is this all there is to us? Although many materialists and atheists will argue that this is so, no-one in his right mind can really agree with such a simplistic definition of man. If we care to think only just a little further than our noses, we very quickly come to realise that somewhere "inside" of us is an indwelling being that not only controls our physical body, but also our emotions and our thoughts. Yet, who is that inner being? That inner being is what we have termed our awareness, that part of our dreamer which is in incarnation. I say "that part of" because the total dreamer is the total awareness of the spirit being, but remember that during incarnation the spirit being manifests only one polarity of its awareness in terms of manhood or womanhood.

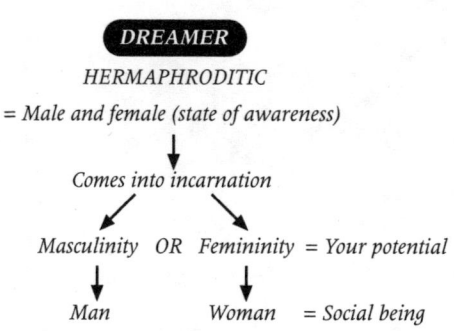

There are many different ways in which we can view the tonal, but for the purposes of this book we are going to look at only one of these definitions. Essentially the tonal is *every-thing* we know ourselves to be, for even that part of our awareness which controls our physical body, emotions and thoughts, must also be part of the tonal, or incarnated being. Of the other polarity of our awareness, and of the spirit being itself, we know nothing. Therefore, for the sake of clarity, we term the tonal *every-thing,* and we term the spirit being, which is the nagal, *no-thing,* simply because from our angle as physical beings the spirit is nothing we know. Thus we have:

NAGAL = NO-THING
TONAL = EVERY-THING

What is implied in the above is quite obvious, namely that the tonal is *life in manifestation*, whilst the nagal is *life unmanifest*.

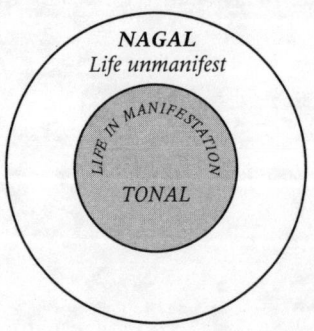

MAN = SPIRIT BEING

NAGAL/SPIRIT = MASCULINE

    ↑   = No body, emotions
* INTERACTION   or mental ability
    ↓   = Nothing

TONAL   = FEMININE

             = Social being
             = Body and emotions
               and mental faculties
             = Everything

* The interaction between spirit and tonal, masculine and feminine, leads to the evolution of awareness

This brings us back to the concept of potential, for clearly the sole purpose of manifestation is to unfold potential, i.e., the spirit incarnates as a result of wanting to explore its own potential. Therefore not only is the spirit the source of all manifested life, but it also pervades the whole of that manifested life. Keeping this as simple as possible, we say that the spirit manifests so as to get to know aspects of itself which it does not yet know, namely, its potential. However, in order to do this, it obviously has to separate the known from the unknown. This means that the spirit has to separate that which it knows about itself from that which it does not yet know.

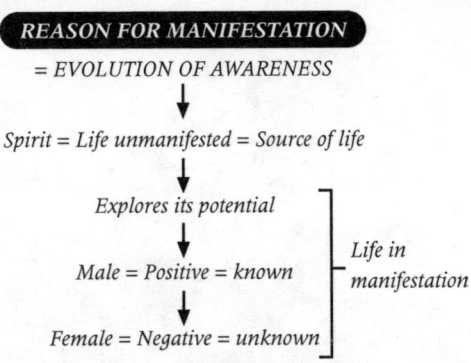

That which is the known implies knowledge which can be utilised, and is like having money in the bank – having a positive bank balance. On the other hand, that which is unknown is like one's potential earnings, which, being only potential, cannot be used until they have been materialised in some way and have been incorporated into one's bank account. This is much like pulling off a business deal so as to earn extra income – until such time as that deal has paid off in terms of hard cash, the potential income from that deal is exactly that, namely, potential. Therefore if the known is like a positive bank balance, then relative to the known, the unknown is as yet negative, meaning that it is still pending. Thus we have:

KNOWN = POSITIVE
UNKNOWN = NEGATIVE

Now just like any good businessman, the spirit also wants to expand its business, (which is the evolution of awareness), to its maximum potential, in that the spirit wishes to include the unknown within the known. However, remember that the physical being, or the tonal, is in fact every-thing, in that it represents all aspects of manifested life, and therefore it must by definition be both chaos and order, light and darkness, positive and negative, male and female. But clearly, if the evolution of awareness is to proceed intelligently, then even at this level it is necessary for the spirit to separate one polarity from the other. It is this act of separation that gives rise to what Toltecs refer to as the *splitting of the sexes*. Yet in relation to all of this we are still only referring to existence at the level of pure awareness – the awareness of the spirit being.

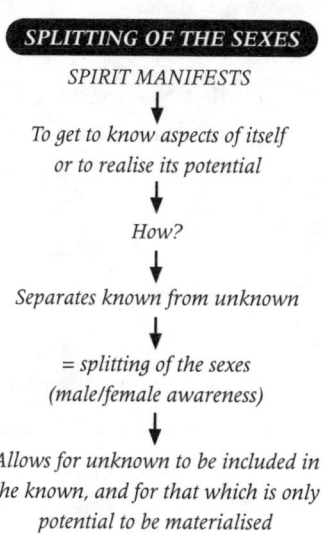

So, it is not a question of one aspect being more important than the other. It is simply a question of having to separate one pole from the other, for the evolution of awareness to proceed unencumbered. Within this process it is also clear why it should be the known that guides and directs the course of evolution, for how else could it be? If the spirit being did not separate the known from the unknown, and then use what it does know in order to unfold more awareness, how could evolution take place? How can we run a business on money we do not have? Therefore when we state that the known is positive relative to the unknown, we are also implying that the tonal is dependent upon the spirit being, not only for incarnation, but also for direction within the course of evolution. To clarify this further let us revert once again to our analogy of owning a business.

If you have your own business, the existence of that business is thanks to you. Without you your business would not exist. Your business is entirely dependent upon the time, the effort and the money you invest in it. The reason why you invest in this business is because it has a great potential, but unless you use your knowledge, unless you use what you know, in order to develop your business, the business will fail. Therefore look upon your business as being the tonal, in which case you are the nagal. Because you are the directing force within that business, you are positive relative to the business.

From this analogy we can see how because of the way in which life works, the tonal is negative relative to the nagal, and why it is also looked upon as being feminine relative to the nagal. Why feminine? Simply because just as it is the male who carries and secretes the life-giving sperm, so too is it the spirit who carries and "secretes" the purpose of life. Without that purpose, without that "sperm," there would be no conception, no birth, and therefore no manifestation or incarnation. This is equally true of you the businessman, because relative to your business you are the male, and unless you direct that business with your purpose, unless you fertilise it with your creative powers, it will fail.

It can of course always be argued that there is no reason why it cannot be the female who provides the purpose, but consider how illogical such an argument really is. Have you ever heard of or encountered anyone who was brought to birth by a business, and whose very existence was then determined by that business? Such an argument is absurd, and is invariably the sign of a distorted mind that upholds the concept of sexual inequality. Although it is true that many people do become the product of their businesses, that is not their origin, and the behaviour of such people is as contrary to the natural order of life as is the behaviour of those who persist in practising sexual inequality. Forever caught up in the idea that to be a male is to be superior to the female, and vice versa, such people are constantly trying to outdo the opposite sex, even in their way of thinking, if it is at all possible to term such trash "thinking!"

From what we have looked at so far, it should not be difficult to see that because the female is negative relative to the spirit, she by definition constitutes for the spirit the unknown which, as we have already noted, is in reality its potential. This potential is of course manifested life, the tonal, and since the tonal is every-thing, light and darkness, male and female, the spirit must of necessity separate one polarity from the other.

The end result of this separation is what we term a physical being that is either a man or a woman, and that has an awareness which is either male or female, and a potential for either masculinity or femininity.

If we look at how things work at the level of the physical plane, we find that the physical being termed "woman" is also negative relative to the physical being termed "man." This is because she has the same relationship to man as female awareness has to male awareness. However, since they are negative, all women are in a very real sense a mixture of order and chaos, light and darkness, male and female, and it is herein that the mystery of the female lies. This mystery is centred around the fact that the female is, in essence, all of these things, for as the representative of the tonal, she is every-thing. This is in direct contrast to the male which, being the representative of the nagal, is no-thing, that is, *the void!* Naturally, the implications here are vast, but they will become rather more clear as we progress.

NAGAL = LIFE UNMANIFEST; NO-THING; THE VOID
TONAL = LIFE IN MANIFESTATION; EVERY-THING;
    THE WOMB

Nevertheless, this does not mean that the male is a nothingness, and that the female is some sort of a freak. Instead it means that the female has a completely different configuration to the male, in that, unlike the male, the female has two distinct sides to her. It is this dual aspect of the female's nature which constitutes for the spirit the unknown. So, from the angle of the male, who is the representative of the spirit, the female is very much a mystery. In fact, if the truth be told, the female is equally a mystery unto herself, even though, generally speaking, women do not like to acknowledge this.

MYSTERY OF THE FEMALE (AWARENESS)

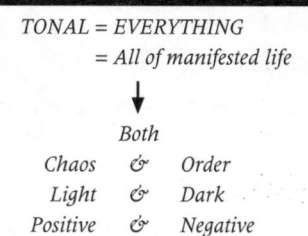

TONAL = EVERYTHING
= All of manifested life

↓

Both
Chaos	*&*	*Order*
Light	*&*	*Dark*
Positive	*&*	*Negative*

Summing up all of the above, we find that all of us are spirit beings with an awareness termed the dreamer. That awareness has two polarities, termed male and female.

Therefore, at this level of existence, we are all hermaphrodites. However, in order to unfold our full potential we need to evolve our awareness, and in order to do so we have to separate the known from the unknown. This brings about the splitting of the sexes and, as a result, and depending upon what our approach to unfolding our potential is to be, we incarnate either the male-side or the female-side of our awareness.

If it is the male-side, then we have a man's body and we approach life from the angle of the spirit, that is, the known. If it is the female-side, then we have a woman's body and we approach life from the angle of the tonal, that is, the unknown. However, in working with the unknown, it is important to remember that until it has been incorporated into the known, it must of necessity be potential. And in being a potential, it is by nature every-thing, positive and negative, light and darkness, male and female, just as within any business there is the potential for both success and failure. Consequently, as spirit beings we have no physical gender as such, since we are both male and female, the known and the unknown, positive and negative. But if we wish to unfold our full potential, then we must manifest that potential. This means that we must incarnate onto the physical plane. In doing so we effect the splitting of the sexes, with the result that we incarnate either as male or as female, as positive or as negative, as the known or as the unknown.

If we are male, then it is a simple splitting into the known and the unknown. However, if we are female, then that splitting in a sense remains undifferentiated and is still the unknown. This is a fact that is reflected in the sex chromosomes, for if we give to the unknown the value of X, and we give to the known the value of Y, then during the splitting of the sexes the male is determined by XY, whereas the female is determined by XX.

As I mentioned earlier, how all of this really works is far too technical for the purposes of this book, but with at least this very simplistic understanding of the concept of gender we can begin to work consciously with the mystery surrounding the void and the womb.

However, the implications of what we are considering are enormous, and they amount to the fact that, unless the proper interaction, or intelligent co-operation, between males and females takes place, then the evolution of awareness does not proceed intelligently, we get resentment and strife, and we end up with the kind of mess we see in the world today. Because the unknown is a mystery, and will always remain so, the mystery of the female can never be fully solved. Yet, through the constant interaction, or co-operation, between male and female, the unknown can gradually become incorporated into the known. Only in this way can men achieve their full potential of masculinity, and can women achieve their full potential of femininity.

In practical terms this means that the mystery of the female can never be solved, or the potential of the female can never be realised, unless she can be incorporated into the purpose and therefore also the life, of the male. This is because it is the male which constitutes the known, and therefore also order. From this, it follows that if the male is the representative of the spirit, then he must materialise the purpose of the spirit, and so must incorporate the unknown within the known. But this is the same thing as saying that the male must come to understand his polar opposite, the female.

The way in which males and females co-operate in order to make this happen, and realise their full potential, is that the female firstly provides the male with a counterbalance; secondly, complements him in every respect; and thirdly, supports him in claiming his power. In order to get a proper understanding of what this means we will, in the next chapter, first digress for a moment, so as to consider briefly the dual nature of the female.

CHAPTER FOUR

THE DUAL NATURE OF THE FEMALE

WE HAVE ALREADY SEEN that the female is essentially both order and chaos, light and darkness, positive and negative, male and female. Toltecs refer to this dual nature of the female in terms of *the mother* and *the female*. Since a mother, as a result of the relative factor of awareness, is masculine relative to her children, irrespective of their gender, Toltecs term the male in the female *the mother,* and term the female in her simply *the female*.

In any relationship the female can play either the role of the mother, or the role of the true female, and this includes her relationship with men. So, if a woman is a businesswoman and runs her own business, then it is the mother in her, which is masculine in quality, that is running that business. Likewise, if she is a married woman, but finds that she has to make all the decisions, then once again it is the mother in her that is keeping the marriage together. However, realise what this implies, especially in marriages. Quite simply, it means that if your wife is in mother mode, then she does not have a husband, but instead has you for a son! Therefore from your perspective you do not have a wife, but a mother to whom you are like a little boy!

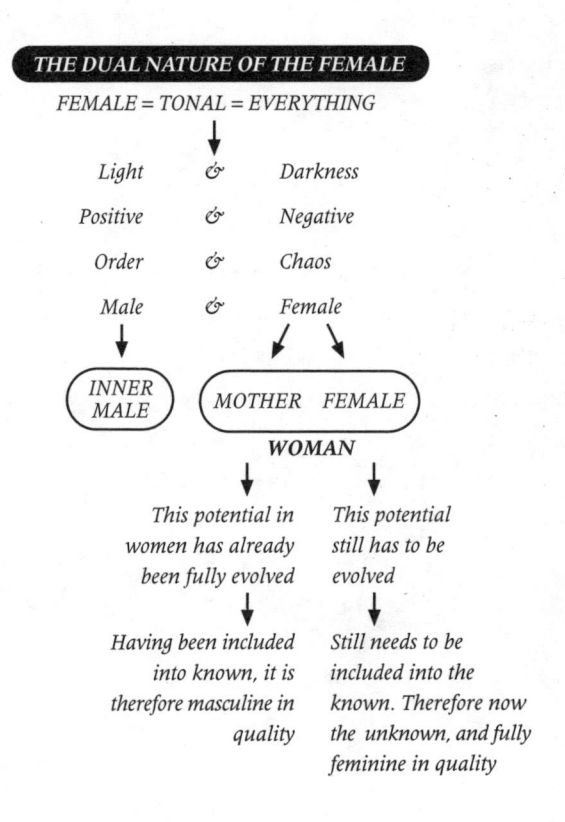

THE DUAL NATURE OF THE FEMALE

FEMALE = TONAL = EVERYTHING

Light	&	Darkness
Positive	&	Negative
Order	&	Chaos
Male	&	Female

INNER MALE

MOTHER   FEMALE

WOMAN

This potential in women has already been fully evolved	This potential still has to be evolved
Having been included into known, it is therefore masculine in quality	Still needs to be included into the known. Therefore now the unknown, and fully feminine in quality

The situation described above is by far the biggest cause of unhappiness and problems within most marriages, because sooner or later the woman begins to tire of having to mother her husband and to have sex with her son, and the man, in his turn, also begins to tire of constantly being told what to do, including when and how to make love to his mother!

The possible results of such a situation are almost unlimited. For example, the husband can start to have affairs with younger women who are less likely to want to mother him, or his wife, for that matter, can start to have affairs with men whom she feels she does not have to mother. The couple can become estranged, or divorced. The man can become aggressive in wanting to dominate his wife as he attempts to assert his maleness, even to the point of becoming violent. The woman can become even more domineering in her efforts to get her husband to enact his true role as the male, with the result that the marriage either deteriorates completely, or the man erupts into physical violence, or just withdraws more and more into himself, becoming evermore the little boy. But in most cases, the problem always arises because the man is not fulfilling his true function as the male, with the result that the female is forced into the role of the mother.

CHAPTER FIVE

SEPARATING MYTH FROM REALITY

Although ignorance begets myth, we cannot afford to forget that all reality is masked by myth. Therefore care must be taken not to discard the baby with the bathwater.

IF YOU LOOK AT YOURSELF, and then at every other man around you, you will quickly see that precious little of what you think you know about what it means to be a male is what you may rightfully claim as being your own knowledge, gained through your own experience. In fact, if you really want to be honest with yourself, you will have to admit that most of what we think we know about ourselves is based entirely upon two things; the first relating to our physical existence; and the second concerning the information fed to us through our social conditioning.

Think for a moment. Who and what are you? Realise that you are not your name. Your name only serves to identify you by virtue of the fact that you have a physical body. If you did not have a physical body you would not have a name, neither would you be a man, a husband, a father, an engineer, or anything else. However, you are not your body! As we saw earlier, neither are you your thoughts or emotions, because you can control all of these.

Regarding the second point, we can equally see that none of the information we have been fed through our social conditioning does anything towards informing us about who and what we really are. All of this information is based entirely upon other people's perceptions and beliefs, most of which have their basis in misconception and prejudice. What's more, the sole purpose of being fed this information is to condition all of us, firstly, into accepting the prejudices of others; and secondly, into having to conform to the biased actions of the majority. The rationale here being that the majority must be right, and the individual must be wrong, unless he or she conforms with what the majority wants.

Consequently, if we are going to get to grips with what is entailed within the mystery of gender and, more specifically, if you are going to grasp what it means to be a true male, then we are going to have to sift through everything we think we know, in order to be able to separate myth from reality. I say sift, because it is important to bear in mind that everything, even the most outrageous fantasies, at some time had the basis of their origins in reality. Because of this we cannot afford simply to discard everything we know, as a result of the anger we feel at having been conditioned into accepting the lies, the prejudices and the misconceptions of others, for in amongst all of that trash lie the kernels of truth we are seeking.

Nevertheless, I must warn you that in our attempts at separating reality from myth, you will, unless you are a male chauvinist, find yourself wanting to resist a great many of the concepts we come up with. The reason for this is that we are dealing here with the result of a great many generations of suppression, of inequality, of injustice, and of the suffering and the struggle of women the world over to try to free themselves from that humiliation. In view of this, it will all too often appear as if I am trying to force women back into the very suppression from which they are only just beginning to escape. However, I am not trying to force women back in time. Neither am I trying to promote male chauvinism. If you will bear with me, then hopefully, as the contents of this book unfold, you will begin to see that far from trying to suppress the female, I am doing everything I can to ensure her liberation, and to accord to her the acknowledgement and the respect she has been denied for so very long. At the same time I am also attempting to provide men with the necessary clarity they need in order to claim their power as true males.

To return now to separating reality from myth, I must also point out that in this book we cannot possibly address every myth and every issue. Accordingly, I have selected only the nine most commonly-held myths. But if we look at these in depth, we will soon come to see that they are in fact the source of all other myths. By addressing these basic nine myths we gain the necessary insight to enable us to unravel any other myth, by virtue of the fact that all myths have their origins in one or the other of the basic nine premises.

PART TWO

THE NINE MYTHS AND THEIR HIDDEN KEYS

CHAPTER SIX

MYTH ONE
MEN DON'T CRY

As we progress in our study of these myths you will soon begin to notice that the first and last myth are two sides of the same coin, and that the others are merely layers of the stuff the coin is made of. Of all the myths, this first is perhaps the least understood, for its real meaning is that the male cannot be helpless.

The reason why the male cannot afford to be helpless is that the female is negative relative to the male. This means that although the female is not in any way inferior to the male, yet, since she is his polar opposite, her natural tendency is towards preservation rather than progression. In other words, whilst the spirit is tending towards the evolution of awareness, the tonal is tending towards the preservation of evolution. But preservation necessarily implies stagnation of sorts, for the simple reason that you cannot have your cake and eat it! We either stay where we are, or we move forward!

Just to recap briefly, remember that the spirit is life unmanifest, and that it wants to get to know its full potential. In order to do so, the spirit, or the archetypal Adam, if you like, must first separate the known from the unknown. This the spirit does by coming into physical manifestation, and that manifestation is what we term the tonal, that is, the every-thing we see as life in manifestation, or the cosmic Eve. But, as we can see so clearly within this life made manifest, everything tends to preservation, and ultimately to inertia.

In addition, because the tonal is everything, light and darkness, positive and negative, male and female, the spirit must once again differentiate between these two polarities of its manifested awareness, and consequently it brings about the splitting of the sexes. As a result we now have Adam, the male, representing the masculine known, and Eve, the female, representing the undifferentiated and therefore feminine, unknown.

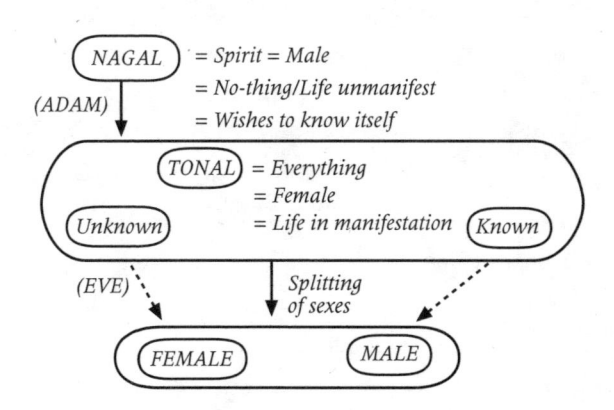

```
       NAGAL      = Spirit = Male
(ADAM)             = No-thing/Life unmanifest
         ↓         = Wishes to know itself

         TONAL    = Everything
                  = Female
  Unknown         = Life in manifestation   Known

   (EVE) ↘     Splitting    ↙
                of sexes

        FEMALE         MALE
```

However, because the male represents the spirit of man, and the female represents the tonal, that is, the physical being of man, it follows that it is only because of the interaction between these two polarities that the evolution of awareness can and does take place. Consequently, in order to evolve its awareness, the spirit must incorporate the unknown, or the female, into the known, for only in this way can the spirit unfold its full potential.

In more down-to-earth terms, this means that deep down inside the heart of every male is the intense desire to get to know his own inner female counterpart, or the tonal, which is life in manifestation. To do so, it is the most natural instinct of the true male to take unto himself a female who will not only be his wife and the mirror of his own inner female, but who will also reflect for him the secrets and the mysteries of life in manifestation.

This is all very well, but if we remember that the tonal is every-thing, that is, chaos and order, light and darkness, positive and negative, and that the female's tendency is towards preservation, then it should be quite clear why the male cannot afford to be helpless. If a man does begin to indulge in being helpless, he only succeeds in calling forth the mother in the female which, as we have already noted, is the masculine aspect of the female. But realise that the mother cannot and will not separate the polarities, for it is neither her function nor her instinct to do so. Therefore the end result of calling forth the mother in the female, is that the female will immediately set about preserving whatever can be salvaged, and in the process will even unconsciously preserve the sense of helplessness in the man concerned!

This is exactly what has happened in the world today. Because men have been acting helpless, the mother in females has taken over, and to such an extent that the world is being dominated by women who are becoming ever more aggressive, as men are becoming ever more weak and self-indulgent. Yet these men also resent mother telling them what to do, when to do it, and how to do it, and as a result, they are becoming more and more like petulant little boys rebelling against everything and everybody, but, just like little boys too, always running away when the shit hits the fan!

So when we look at the world today, we see that humanity has very much become an asexual race in which the individual no longer knows whether he or she should be Arthur or Martha. About the only way in which it is still possible to distinguish one sex from the other is to check out the physical body of the person – although with the marvels of medical science even this is no longer a guarantee! But even so, most of the men who were legitimately born as men still exhibit emotional responses and mental impulses which are truly asexual! And this is equally true of most women today. However, from what we have seen in this book so far, and from what we can also see in the world around us, it should be abundantly clear that this does not work. The only way in which true co-operation and understanding can come about, is for men to be as male as possible, and for women to be as female as possible. In other words, progress can only be made if men strive to be the best males they can be, and if women strive to be the best females they can be. Only in this way can stagnation, or the battle of the sexes, be avoided.

Yet, to give the devil his due, there is a reason why men are tempted to indulge in wanting to be helpless. If we bear in mind that masculinity has its origin in the void, it is not so strange that every man sooner or later begins to wonder how he is ever going to be able to fulfil his fate and unfold his full potential. What starts off within the process of life as being a vague and only partially formulated question, soon enough starts to become a very real fear of failure.

Slowly beginning to realise that everything, including his wife and his family, is his responsibility, and that he has no manual to guide him, every man comes to the frightening conclusion that it is only him and the world out there! In other words, it is up to him, and him alone, to determine whether his life will be successful, happy and fulfilling, or whether it is going to be a nightmare of failure and shame! It is up to him to show the way, to take the lead, and to shoulder the responsibility not only for his own life, but also for the lives of those around him.

And yet, when the man looks within himself to find what he needs, he is faced only with the apparent emptiness of the void. At a very deep level he can sense that the void is not really empty, but his dilemma is that he does not know how to access, much less utilise, the power contained within that inner core of his being. Remember that all of us have been heavily conditioned into being what society believes men should be, but none of us have ever been taught how to tap our true potential as males. We have been taught to think in rational terms, but what good is rational thinking when we have to access the void? We have been taught that men do not cry, but what good is it to be big and brave and strong when deep down inside we feel like a failure?

No male has ever been taught to be a male. And no man has ever been born with a manual on how to claim his power as a male. However, this is the very essence of what it means to be a true male. As a representative of the spirit of man, every man has to find his way by himself, and in doing so, he begins to write his own manual. But find our way to where? Good question! Nevertheless, an invalid question! Why is it invalid? Because by asking questions you are once again acting helpless!

The true male knows that he has only himself, and that he is not going anywhere. Within his heart of hearts he knows there is nowhere to run to, and no-one to turn to. If he needs to go anywhere at all, then it is to search the unknown for the answers he seeks. And if he needs anyone at all, then it is only his own inner female counterpart who represents for him the unknown.

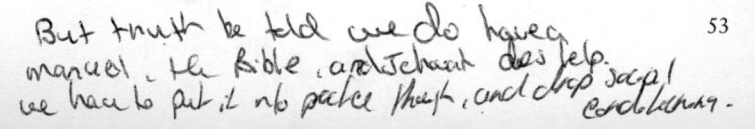

Therefore, far from playing helpless, the true male sets about mapping out the unknown. This he does within himself, as well as within the world out there. By using the female in his life as a mirror for his own inner unknown, the male maps out the unknown within himself, and by using the world around him as a mirror of that greater female termed manifested life, he also maps out the unknown in terms of his fate and his potential. And in doing so, the male gradually finds his way to the void within, and, in time, begins to tap into that endless source of life and creativity.

By getting to know his female counterpart, the male not only maps out the unknown, but also brings it into the light of day by making it conscious knowledge. Through this, the male can then compare that which he already knows about himself with that which he is learning about his unknown potential, and in this way he can bring about any adjustments to his knowledge which may be necessary. In other words, the female brings to the male knowledge which lies beyond his frame of reference.

However, instead of welcoming the knowledge the female brings them, irrespective of whether it is a woman, or that greater female, namely, the world out there, men all too often react very negatively to such input if it does not immediately make logical sense to them. So if a female tells such a man something which sounds irrational, his normal reaction is to think or even to say that she is crazy and has gone off her rocker. But, in doing so, the man is throwing away an opportunity to adjust his knowledge, because the only reason the female's input appears to be irrational, is because she is showing him something outside of his present frame of reference.

Therefore a much more sensible approach is to incorporate the female's input into one's own frame of reference, by adjusting one's knowledge to accommodate this new perspective brought by the female, again, irrespective of whether it is a woman or the world out there. This, after all, is the very meaning of incorporating the unknown within the known, and of solving the mystery of the female by incorporating her into both the purpose and the life of the male. To clarify this, let us look at an example I gave in one of my previous books, *Cry of the Eagle*.

Bill comes home from work one day, and tells his wife, Cindy, that he is concerned that he has not heard from his close friend, Peter, for some time now. Cindy listens to her husband, but after saying that maybe Peter is just too busy to phone Bill as regularly as usual, she launches into a detailed account about the family dog who probably would have drowned in the swimming pool that morning, had she not become suspicious that he was nowhere to be seen.

At face value it appears that Cindy is not particularly worried about Peter, and that her story about the dog has absolutely nothing to do with Bill's concern for his friend. Yet, knowing his wife well enough to be certain that she cares about Peter as much as he does, Bill also accepts that since she told him about the dog, she must somehow feel that this incident has a bearing on Peter's unusual silence, even though right now he cannot for the life of him figure out how the two can possibly be related. However, thinking about his friend, Bill begins to wonder how Peter's business is doing and, without really understanding why, he suddenly feels a sense of unease. Knowing full well that there is no logical reason to feel uneasy about his friend's business expertise, Bill is nevertheless quick to acknowledge that their dog has also never before, in the seven years that they have had him, fallen into the swimming pool.

Feeling alarmed that something may have gone wrong with Peter's business, Bill decides to phone his friend straight away. Speaking to Peter on the phone, Bill is relieved to hear that his friend is well. However, when he asks Peter about his business, Peter tells Bill that he nearly went bankrupt by making a stupid investment in a bogus venture. According to Peter, if it had not been for his female accountant, who sensed that there was something amiss, and insisted that he investigate his partner, he would more than likely have gone bankrupt, as a result of continuing to invest in a venture which did not actually exist!

Bill was fascinated by his friend's story. In all the years he had known Peter, his friend had always been very careful about investing his money. However, this time, like their family dog, Peter had misjudged hopelessly. Had he been unwilling to act upon his accountant's female hunch, then, by his own admission, he would not have suspected that his new partner was up to no good. Peter could easily have waved aside his accountant's hunch as having no foundation, but had he done so, he would have gone under. Bill, likewise, could have dismissed Cindy's story about their dog as being irrelevant to his concern for Peter. But it is clear to see that had either of these two men chosen to ignore the female's input, they would not have incorporated the female into their purpose, and neither would they have mapped out the unknown these females brought them.

Because the male constitutes the known, and therefore also order, it is vital that the male comes to the realisation that, being the physical plane microcosm of the spirit, he cannot afford to indulge in chaos and disorder, any more than he can plead ignorance, play dumb, or act helpless. If he does, then he is not mapping out the unknown, but identifying with it! In other words, instead of coming to grips with his polar opposite, the feminine unknown, he identifies with it, and as a result becomes either like a helpless female, or like an old hen clucking over her brood! I think you know exactly what I mean. I am sure you have come across examples of men who are quite at a loss when they have to change a light bulb, as well as those who will sit and gossip up a storm with the ladies in the canteen!

This is so clear to see in the example above. Had Bill identified with the unknown Cindy was bringing him, he would either have become irritated with her for talking about the dog when he wanted to talk about Peter, or alternatively, he would have started to go off on tangents by talking about the dog, the swimming pool, the hazards of having swimming pools when one has pets, and so on. But had Bill taken either of those two options, the unknown Cindy had brought him would have remained unmapped. In the first instance, by becoming irritated with Cindy, it is more than likely that some kind of argument would have been the result, in which case the unknown would have resulted in chaos and disorder, and possibly even more unanswered questions. In the second instance, the conversation would have gone off on impossible tangents, getting both Bill and Cindy further and further away from finding out what had happened to Peter!

The way in which the evolution of awareness has set it up, is that the male is the one who firstly, provides the lead; secondly, points out the direction; and thirdly, prescribes the method to be employed. These three points are so very important in our understanding of what it is to be a true male that we need to consider each one in depth.

Providing or taking the lead in life does not mean that the male has been given a licence to dominate the female, even though some men seem to think so. By this I am referring to the type of man who quite simply tells the woman what to do, without even vaguely considering that she has her own feelings and perspective on matters. For a man such as this the woman must always be on the ready to do his bidding whenever he demands it, no matter how she feels about it or what she thinks about it. Needless to say, this also means lying down and spreading her legs for him whenever he tells her to do so! For these men, the female is of no real consequence, and neither does that greater female, the world, have any real meaning. Being totally self-centred, these men do not even pause to consider how they rape females and the world around them. Their motto is "Take what you can get, and if you can't get it at first, then demand it, or take it by force!"

Taking the lead means initiating the act, irrespective of

what that act may be. It can be the act of discussing, the act of setting an example of mutual respect, the act of engendering hope, the act of inspiring self-belief in another person, the act of giving guidance to an employee who may be insecure in his or her work, the act of being open to criticism, the act of listening and of taking another person's state of being into account, the act of starting a new project, the act of starting a family, the act of sex, etc. But ultimately, taking the lead means initiating the act of intelligent co-operation.

To understand this, remember that it is the task of the male to get to know his own unknown counterpart, which is not only the female, but also life in manifestation, that is, life upon the physical plane. But in order to do this, the male must have that openness of heart which allows him to interact with both the female and the world in a fully conscious and meaningful way. This means that he must allow and, better still, actively take the female and the world into his space. By taking the female into his space, the male has no option other than to co-operate with her intelligently, for not to do so would mean that he would still end up fighting her, and therefore wanting to overcome and dominate her.

In the example of Bill and Cindy, we saw how this works, for Bill took Cindy into his space by expressing to her his concern about Peter and in addition, he allowed Cindy to be her female self in giving him the only thing she could, namely, the story about the dog. Cindy had no more idea of what had happened to Peter than did Bill, but her female intuition guided her into telling Bill about the dog, even though it is highly unlikely that Cindy herself could see the connection. But because the male is the known, and because he must therefore bring order into the chaos of the unknown, it was very much up to Bill to figure out what Cindy was in fact bringing him. Naturally, exactly the same was true for Peter in his interaction with his female accountant.

Moreover, this example also shows us quite clearly how the female can only get to know herself through the male. But if the female is always being dominated by the male, in that she is being suppressed by him, instead of being allowed into his space as an equal, how can the female ever get to know herself? And this is equally true of the female's greater expression, life upon the physical plane, for it is up to the male to co-operate intelligently with life if order is to be achieved from out of chaos. In fact, the disorder and chaos we see in the world today is entirely the result of men having shunned their responsibility as males and not co-operating intelligently with life or with the female.

Yet, it is not only the men who want to dominate females who cause havoc in the world. Those men who play at being helpless are equally to blame, for in their helplessness and apathy, they throw everything out of balance, and then wonder why the world is falling apart! Realise that whenever the man is acting helpless, the female starts to feel very insecure and, as a result, she will either nag the wretched man to death, or else she will, out of sheer desperation, take on the male role, in which case we revert to the mother and little boy scenario. Therefore whenever men do not act as true males, they are doing an injustice, not only to themselves, but also to the female and the world around them. The consequence of this is that the mother in the female will always come to the rescue, unless she is a complete doormat. But, whenever she does this, the female cannot help but lose her respect for the man.

Instead of just excluding Cindy from his world and phoning Peter without even having spoken to her, or instead of acting helpless by telling Cindy that she must find out what has happened to Peter, Bill behaved like a true male. Taking the lead, Bill pointed out to Cindy that he was concerned about Peter, and after letting Cindy express herself, Bill again took the lead by not allowing either of them to go off on tangents, or to become involved in an argument. Then by taking into consideration how Cindy herself felt about Peter, and also what she told him about the dog, Bill again took the lead by using this as a starting point to co-operate intelligently with his wife in mapping out the unknown.

The second point, namely, pointing out the direction, is really a matter of keeping the focus, and of guiding the female in the right direction. In our example we see that Bill did this by listening to Cindy's story about the dog, but then still keeping the focus on Peter, rather than precipitating an argument or a useless discourse on pets and swimming pools.

We find this a most important point when we consider life in general, for just like Cindy, the world is very much a female. For example, a man wants to sell mugs, but when he speaks to his prospective clients they begin to ask him if he also sells cups and saucers, and did he know that someone else is selling coffee pots, and does he sell coffee pots too, and what about milk jugs and coffee creamers, and can the mugs also be used for soup, and are they microwave-proof, and did he know that microwave products are now really the in-thing, etc.? Clearly, unless this man keeps his focus, he will, in his efforts to please his customers, be so busy trying to source and sell something different every day, that he will more than likely never sell much of anything!

Nevertheless, since he is up against the unknown, the male must also be constantly open to the guidance he is receiving from the female, including the world around him. So, if he is trying to sell mugs, and he gets all of this feedback, then he must decide what to do with it. Either he is getting this feedback because mugs in themselves are not a viable business, and therefore he needs to stock a greater range of products, or else it means that he must stock the best and the largest range of mugs possible! Obviously in this particular case, the easiest and the quickest way for the man to figure out what direction he should take, is not only to monitor his sales, but also to initiate an intelligent co-operation with his clients in the sense of listening to their comments and needs. However, once he has a clear picture of his market, the man will have to decide for himself how best to build his business. By doing this he will be pointing out the direction, in that his customers will then know exactly what product they can buy from him.

Although in this example it is easy to see how the male is expected to point out the direction, there are a great many instances in life where this is not always so clear to see. For example, let us say that Gus, Brad's son, has a problem choosing which subjects he should take in standard six. Brad has two options open to him. Firstly, he can simply order his son to take the subjects which he feels Gus should be taking in order to get a good education; or secondly, he can co-operate with his son intelligently by trying to work out what will be the best for the boy in view of what Gus wants out of his life. If Brad adopts the first approach, he will simply be dominating his son, but the problem facing both father and son, if Brad goes for the second option, is that Gus is still very immature and has absolutely no idea what he would like to pursue in terms of a career.

If Brad is a true male he will not want to dominate his son, and yet he has to take the lead in deciding upon the subjects, and he also has to point out the direction to be taken. How is he to do so? Had Gus been more decisive in terms of possible careers, it would have been easy for Brad to guide his son. However, in this particular case, Brad has no option other than to start mapping out the unknown. There are several ways in which Brad could do this, but for the sake of clarity we will consider only one.

Putting aside his own wishes for what he would like for his son, Brad considers Gus very carefully, and comes to the conclusion that all in all his son is a shy, withdrawn and somewhat timid boy, and who is showing no sign of ever growing out of that introversion. Therefore a career that is highly competitive is not likely to be to his son's benefit. On the other hand, Gus is excellent at mathematics and English, and loves animals and nature. Therefore mathematics and English are already two good choices, and because of his love for animals and nature, botany would be another good choice, and possibly either general science or biology. But when he studies the academic curriculum, Brad notices that if Gus took general science in standards six and seven, he could always switch to biology, zoology, physics or chemistry in standard eight, whereas if he took biology now, he would not be able to switch to either physics or chemistry later on. Therefore in the light of how uncertain Gus is, Brad points out to him that it would be better if he first chose general science, and then decided later which of the other four he would prefer. That still leaves having to choose between English literature, French, Latin, geography, history, art and woodwork.

Brad feels that if Gus were to pursue a career in the sciences, then geography would stand him in good stead, as would Latin. But if he were to decide to pursue instead an academic career in any of the teaching professions, he would be better off with perhaps Latin and history. When he discusses this with his wife, Claire, she points out that she has the feeling that Gus should also learn to overcome his shyness, and therefore he should perhaps not be encouraged to go into a purely academic career in which he could simply lose himself behind his books. Thinking about this, Brad recalls that part of the geography course in standards six and seven also includes group participation in field projects, which would certainly help Gus to overcome his shyness in mixing with others. Geography therefore seems to be a good choice for now, especially since there is nothing to stop Gus from changing to history later should he wish to do so.

Furthermore, students also have the option of changing from woodwork to either of the secondary languages at standard eight level, and bearing in mind what Claire feels, Brad can see that woodwork, being a far more interactive and practical subject than art, would also help Gus to overcome some of his shyness. Having made those choices, it is also clear that Gus should take Latin straight away, as well as English literature. Because Brad has discussed each step of the way with Gus, he does not find it difficult to persuade his son that the subjects he has selected are the best choice for him. Gus can see that in going with this choice of subjects now, he will have a lot of scope for changing subjects later, once he is clearer on what career he would like to pursue, and, in addition, he can also see the wisdom in his father's guidance.

I have chosen to work through this particular example in detail, not only to demonstrate what it means to point out the direction, but also to make it clear that pointing out the direction has nothing to do with violating another person's freedom. The true male will never violate another person's freedom, but will always try to get that person to co-operate intelligently with him. Yet, had Gus not wanted to take Brad's guidance in the choice of subjects, then for his son's own good, Brad would have had to exercise his authority and greater vision in enforcing that choice. Nonetheless, realise that any such enforcement of authority will always be for the benefit of the other person concerned, and never because the male is wanting to impose his will upon that person.

Our third point under consideration is the fact that the male prescribes the method to be employed. In many ways this point grows out of the previous two, in that it also has its basis in the act of intelligent co-operation. The best way in which to explain this is to say that, as a rule of thumb, the male will always, firstly, take the lead by initiating the act of intelligent co-operation; and secondly, ascertain the required direction. This he does, so as to be able to formulate the method to be employed. In order to grasp this fully, let us again consider the example of Brad and his son.

Being the alpha male in his household, the education of his son is primarily Brad's responsibility, even if Gus had not come to him for guidance in choosing his subjects. Therefore if Gus had not approached his father, Brad would have had to take the lead by initiating the act of intelligent co-operation with Gus in trying to figure out why his son had not chosen to consult him. It could be that Gus was perfectly mature and wise enough to make his own decisions without help from his father. But even if that had been the case, it would then still be Brad's responsibility to point out to his son that all of life is interrelated, and therefore fully interactive and interdependent. This he would have done by spelling out to Gus that whilst he still lives at home, and whilst Brad is paying for his education, his parents do have a vested interest in his future as well as his career. To exclude his parents from his decision-making not only implies a lack of respect and trust, but it also smacks of arrogance, coupled with an attitude of self-centredness. Brad would certainly be failing in his task as a father if he allowed his son to develop such an attitude and behaviour.

In this particular case, the direction Brad would have chosen is to give his son a lesson in respect for the world around him, and the meaning of the interrelationship of life. But the method he would have employed would more than likely have been one of, gently but firmly, making it quite clear to his son that he will not tolerate such a display of disrespect. Therefore, in one simple lesson, Brad would have guided his son into a deeper understanding of the need for intelligent cooperation, and would thereby have helped him greatly in growing up to be a true male.

But in our example, we portrayed Gus as being very insecure in his decision-making, and so he came to his father for help. As we saw, Brad did not dictate to his son, for had he done so, he would have dominated Gus by imposing his will upon him, and he would also have failed to teach his son that a male cannot afford to be helpless. By encouraging Gus to cooperate intelligently with him in making the correct choice of subjects, Brad worked through everything step by step with Gus, even by showing him how to include the female, in this case, his mother, in working out the direction to be followed. The whole exercise was therefore not just a matter of choosing school subjects, but was very much in the nature of teaching Gus how the male can overcome the sense of helplessness by tackling the problem one step at a time, in the simplest and most practical manner possible.

From these two scenarios it should now be clear that the method to be employed depends upon the needs that are created by the situation. In both cases the face value of the situation was the issue of Gus having to choose his school subjects, but each scenario brought forth different needs. Yet, in each, we can also see that the true male does not dominate, or impose, or violate, but stands firm and unwavering in his knowledge and in his responsibility of being the male. Never can the male afford to be helpless, to dither, to doubt, and to vacillate this way and that. If he does, he will become either a whimpering coward who believes that everyone and everything is out to get at him, or a domineering brute who goes out of his way to dominate and suppress everyone and everything in his fear of competition. In both cases he will be truly ineffectual as a male, even if he does manage to get people to do his bidding, either through manipulating them into feeling sorry for him, or through frightening them into submission. Whilst in the first case he will be too busy bowing and scraping like a beggar to make any real difference in the world, in the second case he will be too busy bullying to notice that no-one is co-operating with him. The true male, on the other hand, is loved and respected by all, and as a result finds himself to be a natural leader, simply because people instinctively feel that by taking his lead they become uplifted, and this naturally includes the female in such a male's life.

In our treatment of this myth, we have also laid the foundation for the other eight, and therefore, not only will we be able to cover the remaining myths rather more quickly, but we will also begin to see how interrelated they all are. What will help you greatly throughout our study of the myths is if, at the end of each, you make for yourself a list of all the ways in which you fail to live according to the information imparted. If you do this, you will very quickly come to realise why, and once that much is clear, you will be well on your way to being able to change yourself and your ways. Remember, knowledge of the self is true power!

CHAPTER SEVEN

MYTH TWO
MEN ARE AGGRESSIVE

I F WE LOOK AT this second myth in relation to what we have learned so far, it is not difficult to see that the deeper meaning here is that the male must be prepared to fight. This, of course, does not mean that the male must involve himself in a fist brawl on the pavement or in a bar, but rather that the male must set the example in walking the Path of Freedom. Therefore let us first of all consider what is meant by "walking the Path of Freedom."

There are a great many interpretations of what constitutes freedom, and as a result there are also an almost unlimited number of ways in which we can define the meaning of this term. But for the purpose of this book we are going to define freedom as being "the ability of the male to act impeccably upon his own knowledge without fear." Even after just a little thought, the implications of this definition are immediately obvious and vast.

The most important of these is that not every man has the ability to act. As with any ability, we either have that ability, or we do not. If we have the ability to act, that is good; if we don't have it, we have to acquire it. Although this may appear to be overly-obvious, realise that very few people really ever act in the true sense of the word. Most people simply re-act or, more precisely, re-enact their normal behaviour, over and over again. For example, I punch you on the nose, and you react according to your normal behaviour. If you are aggressive, you will punch me back. If you are timid, you will feel extremely hard-done-by, and will accuse me of being a bully.

However, in both cases you will not be acting, but simply reacting according to your normal behaviour, and if I too am only capable of reacting, rather than acting, I will in turn also react to your reaction. Therefore if you punch me back, we will more than likely end up having a full-blown fist fight. But if you feel hard-done-by and try to give me a tongue-lashing, I will probably keep on manhandling you until you either shut up or make good your escape!

The true male, on the other hand, will never react, no matter what, for the moment we react we are out of control. So if I punch Jim, who is a true male, he will, just like anyone else, become exceedingly angry, but he will also use that anger to fight according to the needs called forth by the issue at hand. However, I am not given to just punching people willy-nilly and, being a true male, Jim will be acknowledging this fact, no matter how out of control I am. Therefore, rather than embroiling us both in any further reactions, Jim will immediately strive to bring me back to a state of clarity in which I can control myself. If I am reasonable enough to talk to, Jim will talk me back into my senses, and will more than likely make me feel so guilty for what I have done, that I will become meekness itself. If, on the other hand, I am so out of control that I cannot be reasoned with, Jim is likely to hit me so hard when I least expect it, that I will have no option other than to listen to him, if I am not to risk having my kneecaps smashed and my neck broken. Once I am listening, Jim will make sure that he gets his message across to me quite clearly and, as before, I will have learned that a true male does not fight as a reaction, but in order to remain fully in control of his behaviour.

I always like to use this example because, although it demonstrates the difference between action as opposed to reaction, it also invariably opens up a wonderful can of worms! Immediately, I get delicious reactions like, "What if the man is much bigger than I am?" "What if it is a gangster who has me at gun-point?" "What if it is a woman who is hitting me with her handbag?" "What if this, that or the other?"

I simply laugh quietly and point out to the man concerned that not only is he behaving like a helpless little boy who has to be told what to do, but that he is also reacting so on cue to what I have said! No! The true male is never helpless, and never allows himself to react, no matter what!

Therefore, if I am having to deal with a man who is out of control and twice my size, I will make sure that I act in such a way that he will never have the chance to hit me back. How I do this will depend upon the circumstances and what I have at my disposal in that moment. If the man is out of his mind, and I have nothing but my bare hands, I have no option other than to rely upon sharp wits and a smooth tongue to win enough time to calm the man down. Likewise, if I am being held at gun-point by a gangster, I will act in such a way that I am able to stay alive long enough to overcome him in some way, if not now, then at some later stage. If I am being beaten up by a woman with her handbag, I am certainly strong enough to ward off her blows and to restrain her. But the bottom line is that by not simply reacting to the situation, the true male can and will find a way to act absolutely impeccably, and in such a way that he can fight back in a truly knowledgeable and meaningful manner.

Nevertheless, realise that it is only possible for the male to do this when he stands free from his fear. All of us are subjected to fear, and in this respect none of us are ever truly free from fear, but it is possible for us to stand free from fear in the sense of being detached from it. Being detached from fear is a far cry from submitting to it. Whenever we submit to our fear, we become debilitated by that fear, and therefore instead of being in control, we find ourselves reacting impulsively to every demand made upon us. Yet, when we stand detached from the fear, we can use it to remain fully alert and highly responsive to every little bit of help we are able to rustle up from out of the situation. By doing this, we can act in such a manner that we always will gain the upper hand in some way.

Consequently, we either submit to our fear and react, or we use our fear to act impeccably! This is true, irrespective of what the fear may be. For example, if I fear being made a fool of, I have two options open to me when someone is trying to make me appear a fool. I can either submit to that fear, and start reacting defensively, or I can use that fear to act impeccably. If I react defensively, I will only be goading the other person into continuing to make me appear and feel like a fool. If, on the other hand, I act impeccably, I will find my gap to turn the tables on my opponent, in which case he will be the one to end up feeling downright foolish!

Likewise, if I fear physical pain, and someone threatens to punch me, I can either submit to that fear and run away like a coward, or I can detach from my fear and stand my ground. If I now use my fear to be hyper-alert to any punch which that man may want to swing at me, the chances are that I will be able to avoid it in time. But in that state of alertness, I will also be able to see my gap to being able to handle him in some way, either physically or verbally.

In everything we have looked at so far, the huge difference between acting as opposed to reacting should be quite apparent, as should the real meaning of what it is to fight. Any old fool can react with utter abandon, swinging wild punches and uttering foul oaths, but it takes a real inner fight to remain impeccable enough to fight back with the inner knowledge that adds meaning, and therefore impact, to the male's action. Any male who has mastered that inner fight is truly a free being. Standing detached from both fear and reaction, he is at liberty to act upon his own knowledge, and he alone will be the judge of his level of impeccability. That is true freedom, and the true male is always an example for everyone of what it means to walk the Path of Freedom.

This brings us to another of the implications we have to consider here, namely, knowledge. Remember that knowledge is power that we have gained through our own personal experience. Therefore when we look at the fact that the male fights for the freedom to act upon his own knowledge, the question that comes up is, "What exactly do we mean by this?"

To put it in a nutshell, knowledge or power means having the right values in life. Power does not mean having power over others, in the sense of being able to manipulate them, or being able to kill them, or victimise them in some other way. Power means that the knowledge you have at your disposal makes you more or less invincible, depending upon how much power you have at your command. This means that your knowledge is such that others cannot manipulate or victimise you. Yet such knowledge can only be real power if it is based upon the right values in life, for it stands to reason that if your values are wrong, you will not be invincible at all!

What then do we understand by "right values?" This is a concept which we can make as complicated or as simple as we like. From my perspective it is simplicity itself. The right values are those which are life-supporting, because they lead to freedom and growth, whereas the wrong values are life-destructive, because they lead to bondage and decay. For example, those people who are for ever sitting on the fence and never wanting to rock the boat, are what I call Mr. Nice Guys. But a Mr. Nice Guy will support anything, even his worst enemy's bullshit, simply because he does not want to create waves! Yet by taking that stance, Mr. Nice Guy encourages the people around him to do as they please, irrespective of how destructive their actions may be. Therefore although Mr. Nice Guy may believe that he has the right values in life, in that he doesn't interfere in other people's business, and doesn't dictate to them, his so-called right values are actually leading to chaos and disorder, crime and violence, and possibly ultimately to anarchy. In fact, Mr. Nice Guy will be so concerned about not violating people's freedom, that he will even allow his own son to become a drug addict and a gangster! But how can we maintain that such values are right?

What makes a value right or wrong, are not the moral implications, but the results of living by that value. This is so clear to see in the example above, for although Mr. Nice Guy is saying all the right words concerning freedom, he is, through his actions or rather, lack of actions, encouraging anything but freedom! For me freedom does not mean that every Tom, Dick and Harry can run around terrorising and victimising people in the neighbourhood! Therefore, from my perspective, the effects of being a Mr. Nice Guy can hardly be termed life-supporting.

The true male, on the other hand, will only uphold those values which he knows from his own personal experience do actually lead to freedom, not only for himself, but also for those around him. In other words, the right values are simply those which create an environment in which everyone and everything are able to be safe, to grow and flourish, and to be happy and content. However, the question that is always raised here is, "Who gives us the right to decide what is good for someone else?" The answer is simple: "None of us have the right to impose our will upon others!" But realise that this works both ways.

Although I cannot impose my will upon you, you also have absolutely no right to want to impose your will upon me! Therefore if I want to create an environment which is life-supporting, and you want to create one that is life-destructive, then that is fine, but just make sure you stay out of my way, and out of the way of those around me. If you don't, you will find yourself at the sharp end of my sword! It is as simple as that. I will always fight for the freedom to act upon my own knowledge, and if you wish to be in my space, then that means you will have to reassess your values! My values are tried and tested, and have proved themselves to be truly life-supportive, and thus I cannot possibly stand accused of wrong action. Many people have tried, and no doubt will continue to try, but it is hard to fight the truth!

Yet another of the implications that arises here, is that by having the right values in life, the true male takes the lead in showing all around him how best to achieve freedom from social conditioning. Although this is a major implication, I do not believe we need to belabour it, for it speaks so very clearly for itself. How can we ever be truly free if we always bow down to the dictates of society? How can we ever act upon our own knowledge, if we can only react on the basis of what we have been conditioned into believing? How can we ever have the right values, if we can never think and decide for ourselves what is right or wrong? But, most important of all, how can we ever claim our power as males, if we remain trapped in what we have been conditioned into believing men should be?

The true male is a being who has learned to fight a long hard battle at standing sufficiently detached from his fear, so as to step out of the circle of social conditioning. But to remain standing free from that conditioning is no easy task, for again and again is he challenged, not only regarding his actions, but also his belief in self. Time and time again is the male forced to re-evaluate and to reassess his knowledge, his stance, his actions and, above all, his belief in himself. Never can he afford to become complacent, or over-confident, or self-righteous, for if he does, he immediately becomes vulnerable to attack. Only by standing tall and proud in his own knowledge, knowing within his heart of hearts that he is for ever open and alert, for ever ready to re-adjust his knowledge so as to include the unknown within his present frame of reference, can the male feel secure in fighting that never-ending battle against submitting to the pressure of social conditioning.

Nevertheless, to stand firm in one's own knowledge, without becoming complacent, over-confident, or self-righteous, is only possible because the male is always willing and ready to confront, first of all, himself, and secondly, others. Note the order of this confrontation; first yourself, and only then others. Realise that unless you can honestly trust your own knowledge and your own judgement, you will not be able to stand firm in that knowledge. If you cannot believe in yourself, then how can you expect others to believe in you, especially females? Similarly, if you cannot stand firm in your knowledge, then what security do you offer anyone around you, and how can you expect the female to take your lead?

It is only by confronting ourselves continuously at all levels, physically, emotionally and mentally, that we can gain a belief in ourselves, our knowledge and our judgement. By checking our actions, by questioning our emotions, by evaluating our feelings, and by assessing our thoughts on an ongoing basis, we learn to adjust and to re-adjust our knowledge so that we ourselves can begin to see its value. Once true value begins to emerge, and once we can see it for ourselves, then we also have the right to start confronting those around us, so that they too can begin to acquire that honesty with self that ultimately leads to true freedom.

CHAPTER EIGHT

MYTH THREE
MEN MUST BE EDUCATED

THE REAL MEANING of this myth is that the male must have knowledge, the importance of which we have already been noting, in that real knowledge, as opposed to mere information, is true power. But when we refer to power, we should also know that there are two kinds of power. The first kind is knowledge gained in previous lifetimes. This is what we normally perceive as gifts, talents, abnormal ability or even genius. The second kind is the evolution of new knowledge in this lifetime. It is the sum of both of these types of power or knowledge that constitutes our potential.

So if we consider what is called education, we see that this should involve teaching us not only how to evolve new knowledge, but also how to materialise the knowledge already gained in previous lives. In this respect, even though talent is knowledge gained in previous lifetimes, it must still be nurtured and developed, just like any ability, before we can utilise it fully.

Consequently, when we consider our power or knowledge, we must keep in mind that the only knowledge that we can use consciously is that which we have gained in this lifetime. Knowledge gained in previous lifetimes may well be a natural talent, but until such time as we can consciously use it, the talent remains just beyond our reach. In other words, an undeveloped talent in a person will enable him to sense what he needs to do, and how to do it, but unless he trusts himself to act upon that feeling, it will be of no good to him.

So, what we keep coming back to is that all knowledge gained through experience is true power, for knowledge is something that can be used in the moment, and anything that can be used gives one power in one way or another. For example, if you have money in the bank, you have got financial power. If you have knowledge of politics, you will have political power, should you choose to use that knowledge. But our undeveloped talents or abilities are also power, even though they may as yet be untapped. Therefore, irrespective of whether we come into this lifetime already showing great talent for developing a particular ability, or whether we find that we have to work hard at developing that ability, we all have power at our command.

Earlier we talked about using and acting upon feelings. What do we mean by feelings? Firstly, we should know that feelings are not the same as emotions. There are only four pure emotions, and these are joy, anger, fear and melancholy. Secondly, there are two types of feelings. The first is that type we noted earlier, and which is the expression of latent ability. This type of feeling is in the nature of a person being able to sense what he needs to do, and even how to do it. The second type is more in the nature of guidance received from the world around us. But both types are an expression of irrational knowledge, for there is no logical explanation as to how we arrived at that knowledge. This is what I term listening to the heart, or using one's intuition, or following one's gut feel.

However, although we have all been taught, or rather, encouraged, to rationalise, none of us have ever been taught to listen to our hearts. Listening to the heart means listening to our gut feel, and then acting upon those feelings, rather than acting upon rational assumption. The rational mind is in fact only the human being's own inbuilt computer and, just like any computer, it is only as good as the information stored in it. But the information stored in the computer, in the rational mind, is what constitutes one's view of the world. This view of the world is based mostly upon preconceived ideas and prejudices, and is therefore quite literally the way in which we have become conditioned into looking at everything in our lives, including what it is to be male.

Because people have become conditioned into living in their heads, that conditioning, which is part of their view of the world, has had the effect of breeding in them the desire to rationalise, in an attempt to justify wrong action. As a result, few people really know how to listen to their hearts. Instead they engage in endless internal chatter that goes round and round in the mind indefinitely. But clearly, that internal chatter has got nothing to do with listening to your heart.

As paradoxical as it may appear, listening to the heart, as opposed to rationalizing, is in fact what constitutes true thinking. The academics of this world do not like to admit it, but the truth of the matter is that all so-called "great minds" act upon feeling. Irrespective of whether it is a new invention, a remarkable discovery in science, a musical composition or a great work of art, the creativity that has led to such works has its origin in feeling. Only once that feeling has been translated into a mental vision of what can be, does the inventor, scientist, composer or artist use the rational mind to work out the practicalities involved in materialising his vision.

When we try to listen to the heart it is crucial that we cultivate the good habit of always looking upon our life as one whole, that has both meaning and purpose. If we do not do this, then our life always appears to be a mixed bag of unrelated mishaps and luck that seems to make no real sense at all, and if we see our life in terms of a mixed bag of odds and sods, then it is clear that we cannot possibly glean any real sense of purpose, let alone gain a vision of our fate. So we need to take stock of all of our life's experience. In so doing, we must keep striving for that openness of heart that allows us to sense, to feel, the connecting threads running throughout our life. These threads will not only point out clearly what is really taking place in our lives, but they will also inspire in us the sense of purpose that will ultimately lead us into fulfilling our fate. In addition to these threads, we are always surrounded by more than enough guidance from the world around us. Therefore, all we have to do in following the threads, is to listen to this guidance, by not allowing our view of the world to close us off from what we can sense is our purpose and our fate.

However, even though everyone has feelings, the majority of men do not pay heed to their feelings, not so much because they do not want to, but simply because they do not trust their feelings enough to act upon them. To understand this, it may help if we look at a simple example.

Let us say that you are in the process of applying for a new job. Now the fact is that, irrespective of how much you already know about the job, you will not know exactly what it entails until you are actually doing it. But you would not have applied for this job if you did not have the feeling that it was the right kind of job for you. Therefore all that you can do, is just to trust that feeling, otherwise you will never take the job.

Now, if you trust your feelings concerning this job, in the sense that not only does it feel right to you, but also that you feel strongly compelled to accept it, the chances are that this job is going to be your dream job. But if you have the feeling at the outset that you are not so sure if you are really going to like the job, then rest assured that if you do accept this job, you will end up hating it, for you will soon enough find out that it is not what you had expected or hoped for.

Yet, what all too often causes problems here, is that the majority of people have never taken the trouble to distinguish between logical assumption and feeling. As a result, the rational mind will always tend to interfere in the process of making decisions that have been prompted by feeling. For example, you may well feel that this is the right job for you, but then the rational mind will kick in with objections like, "Well, the salary is not too good, and I don't see that I stand much chance of promotion in this company." In other words, your mind is interfering in your decision by asking of you, "Is this really the right job?" However, the chances are that if you do feel this is the right job, and you go with it, then in no time at all you will get a salary increase, and the opportunity for promotion will also materialise in one way or another.

In working with feelings we should bear in mind that not all feelings are positive. People do not as a rule like negative feelings, and as a result they try to push them away. Yet there is nothing wrong with having negative feelings. Often it is only because of our negative feelings that we can circumvent possible disasters. Therefore, in listening to one's heart, we should never push away our negative feelings, for it stands to reason that life cannot consist of only positive experiences. So as not to have gaps in our knowledge, and in order to bring out our full potential, we also need negative experiences, and such experiences will always be preceded by negative feelings.

When it comes to practising listening to the heart, remember these two important points. The first is that, deep down inside, if only we pay attention to it, all of us can always feel what is right and what is wrong, what is working and what is not. The second is that we all have more than enough guidance from the world around us to enable us to overcome any challenge in our lives. But in order to use the guidance we must have that honesty which constitutes a true openness of heart. If we remember these two points, there will never be a need or an excuse to rationalise – instead we will find ourselves thinking clearly, and acting with utter impeccability.

The final point we should note with respect to listening to the heart, concerns the male's ability to access the power of the void. We have already seen that listening to the heart is in actual fact true thinking, and that all acts of creation arise from out of a feeling. Yet this doesn't take us very far in exploring a subject which is so vast that I cannot begin to do it justice within the scope of this book. Therefore, the serious reader is encouraged to study this concept in greater depth in my other books. So let it suffice for now to say that true thinking is creative, and that the void is the source of all creativity. However, being nothing, that is, no-thing, it is impossible to access the power of the void through rational means. The only way in which to gain access to the void and to tap the creative power in it, is to use our feelings. It is quite literally a case of having to "feel our way around in the dark," which is much the same thing as saying, "feeling our way around the state of nothingness."

I cannot think of any better way to explain this concept than to quote the words of that great sculptor, Michelangelo. In describing to a friend how he works, Michelangelo said: "I do not decide what to carve from a new piece of marble. Instead I allow my feelings to explore that piece of stone until something in me begins to resonate with what seems to be a vibration of sorts trying to express itself through that stone, and using me as the instrument that will give life to that expression." That "something" Michelangelo is referring to as being within himself, is the void, and the "vibration trying to express itself," is the creative power of the void. "Resonating" with that vibration is the act of becoming conscious of a specific form that can be brought into physical existence by utilising the power within the void.

Accordingly, the key to accessing and utilising the power of the void lies in our ability to listen to the heart, and to allow our feelings to guide us. So the man whose heart is closed, and who therefore cannot utilise his feelings effectively, is completely sterile and, to all intents and purposes, is also impotent. Even though such men are normally exceedingly active sexually, that high sex drive is but a result of a deep inner sense of failure at not being able to be creative in their lives. Being caught up in the sterility born of rational assumption, the only things these men can bring into existence are babies! But realise that no man can feel truly fulfilled when deep down inside he knows that he is merely a sperm donor being used for reproduction!

In the final analysis, reproduction is exactly what the word tells us: "reproduction." And reproduction is not creation! Yet to be a true male means that the man can and does utilise all of his creative power, and this he can only do by accessing the power of the void through the medium of his feelings. Therefore when it is stated that the male must have knowledge, it actually means that the male must be able to make use of irrational knowledge in accessing the power of the void. Although it is undeniably true that all knowledge is power, it is only irrational knowledge that can be utilised for creation. Why? Quite simply because once we have utilised irrational knowledge, we have incorporated it into the known, and since it is only possible to create something once, any repeat must of necessity be a reproduction!

CHAPTER NINE

MYTH FOUR
MEN MUST THINK

THIS MYTH IS very much a continuation of the previous one. We can immediately see that it involves the concept of true thinking, as opposed to rationalisation, but its wider significance is to point out the purpose of thinking, namely, that the male must have a strategy. Therefore, in our consideration of this myth we will be looking at both the meaning and the purpose of having a strategy. However, before we can do this, we first have to digress for a moment, so as to consider the meaning of fate and destiny.

Because many people do not believe in life after death, or in reincarnation, it has become generally accepted that fate and destiny are one and the same thing. Yet this is not entirely so, even though these terms are closely related. Destiny pertains to the evolution of awareness across all of time, and it therefore includes all of countless lifetimes spent in incarnation. Destiny is quite literally the force of evolution relative to the individual unit of the one life. As such it is not only the force that determines the time, the circumstances and the quality of each and every incarnation, but is also the force that guides us throughout each incarnation.

Fate, on the other hand, is that tiny part of our destiny which needs to be worked out and fulfilled in any one particular lifetime. In other words, fate is what we term our purpose, or the purpose of this particular lifetime. So it is quite evident that by not fulfilling our purpose, we miss the point in this lifetime, which means that we will be failing to meet our fate, and that, moreover, we will also be failing to take the next step forward in our destiny.

However, the good news is that in practice it is not possible to miss or to avoid fulfilling our fate, for if this were possible, most of us would spend countless lifetimes involved in meaningless activities that amount to nothing of any significance, and the evolution of awareness would not be able to progress very intelligently. Each and every one of us comes into incarnation to fulfil a specific purpose through the materialisation of a pre-ordained fate and, by hook or by crook, through intelligent co-operation or by default, we end up fulfilling that purpose more or less successfully.

This is much like a child at school who has to pass a certain grade each year. In our journey upon life, each incarnation is like a certain grade, and if we co-operate intelligently with the forces of destiny working out through fate, we will "pass" that grade with flying colours. If, on the other hand, we fight the forces of destiny, we are like delinquent students who have to be forced into learning, and who most of the time manage to learn just enough to scrape together the required "marks" to barely pass the grade. But in order to understand this better, let us look at another analogy.

Let us say that it is your fate to go to Rome in this lifetime. Now the way in which you travel to Rome is your choice. You can walk there, or fly there, or take a boat, a train, or any other form of transport you wish. You may also go straight to Rome, or you may travel from one country to the next on your way to it. But, one way or another, the forces of destiny will keep adjusting the circumstances in your life so as to keep you moving ever closer to Rome. If you wish to co-operate, you can make the journey as rich and exciting and adventurous as you choose. If, on the other hand, you are really stubborn, and you try to avoid going to Rome, you will, in the end, be forced through the circumstances in your life to go to Rome, no matter how much you try to avoid this.

Therefore, in spite of all the debates about this concept, the only so called "free will" we really have, is in how we fulfil our fate. In other words, we either turn the journey to Rome into a fun journey of adventure, or we end up being dragged there by the hair, kicking and screaming and fighting. We either flow with the guidance we receive from life, in which case our fate unfolds smoothly; or we try to ignore that guidance, in which case we find ourselves struggling against a force that never lets up.

If we return now to the concept of having a strategy, it should be starting to become clear that to have a strategy does not mean that we must have a plan. Because none of us can avoid our fate, planning a future is an utter waste of time, for it invariably amounts to nothing more than an exercise in folly. None of us knows what the future holds, and therefore what is the point of making plans which may or may not materialise? Yet, realise that this does not mean that life itself is folly. What constitutes the folly within life, is our preconceived ideas about what we haphazardly believe life should be!

If we are to avoid the folly of making plans that could be way off the mark, the only viable thing to do is to work out a strategy that will enable us to fathom, firstly, what exactly our fate entails; and secondly, how best to fulfil that fate. But, of course, the question that arises here is, "How do we do that?"

Bearing in mind what we learned in the previous chapter about listening to our hearts, it is really not all that difficult to work out what our purpose in this lifetime is. In fact, if we truly wish for guidance, we find that we are always surrounded by more than enough. All we have to do is to make the effort to listen to this guidance, by not allowing our view of the world and our preconceived ideas to get in the way. But this is invariably where the problems lie, for our view of the world is a product of our social conditioning, and is therefore one of the major factors preventing us from being able to recognise our fate. For example, how many times have you tried to be something that is based on society's idea of a successful person? Or alternatively, how many times have you tried to base your life on a dream that you inherited from somebody else?

However, if you make the effort to listen to your heart, then even if your parents convinced you that your path lay in becoming a doctor, or a lawyer, and even if your rational mind saw the logic in this, you will still be able to feel if this was the right decision or not. If it is the right career for you, then, one way or another, you will feel completely fulfilled. But if you just chose this career because of your parents' wishes, and it really does have nothing to do with your fate, you will feel that it is not fulfilling, and that it is somehow wrong.

Likewise, if you find that your lifestyle seems somehow empty and void of any real meaning, then rest assured that your heart is telling you it is time to change your whole approach to life, to your spouse, your friends and, most important of all, to yourself! In other words, your heart is telling you that you must take stock of all of your life's experience, in order to reassess your understanding of those experiences and to re-evaluate your notion of what constitutes a happy and successful life.

Therefore, consider carefully what type of people your parents are. Look at the values you have learned from them, from your siblings and relatives, your teachers at school and your colleagues and friends, both past and present. Look at the type of education you have had. Look at where you have lived, and the circumstances you encountered in those homes, those neighbourhoods and towns. Consider all the people with whom you have had close and meaningful relationships, as well as at your so-called enemies. Look at your career, at your natural talents and abilities. Look at everything in your life, and then ask yourself, "What have I learned from all of this? What has all this learning been preparing me for?"

Everything we learn in life is but the guidance we need to be able to discern our purpose, and in this respect there are no accidents and no co-incidences. Everything has meaning. Everything is needed. All we have to do is strive to be open enough to what is taking place in our lives, so that we can see what it is we are being guided towards, and *that* is always our purpose, and therefore our fate.

Once we know what our purpose in life is, it is really not difficult to ascertain how to fulfil our fate. But, in trying to do this, all of us can only start at where we are right now. By this, I mean that even if you do not know what is your fate, you will quickly enough find out, if you start following your feelings. And to follow our feelings is not difficult or complicated, provided only that we want to follow them, and provided that we translate our wishes into the required action. Following our feelings is as natural as it is to breathe. What stops us from following our feelings is our conditioned impulse to discard feeling in favour of rational assumption. But only you can choose to reverse that impulse.

Once the male has ascertained his purpose in life, and once he has begun to fulfil his fate, he also quite automatically begins to play a vital and meaningful role in the lives of those whose fates are either allied with or attached to his own. This is a most important point which should never be forgotten, for it concerns both the females and the males in one's life.

First of all, remember that because the male is the representative of the spirit, any female's fate is attached to that of one particular male in her life. For the majority of females this male will invariably be her spouse. But for those females who, for whatever reasons, have to follow a fate which does not allow for marriage in this lifetime, the male whose fate will play an active role in the fulfilment of their own, will obviously not be a spouse, but can be any male. In either case, the point to grasp is that the female, being a representative of the tonal, can only fulfil her own fate through either the direct or the indirect influence of a male. The implication here is that unless you fulfil your fate impeccably, you will be hampering, not only yourself, but also the female in your life, whose fate is tied in with yours.

However, by far the worse implication in not fulfilling your true purpose, is that if you have willy-nilly chosen to pursue a purpose that is way off the mark as far as your fate is concerned, the chances are that you will attract women into your life who are wanting to support that false purpose. If you do, then realise that neither you, nor that woman, will be able to keep nurturing a purpose that is not true to your fate, and therefore, sooner or later, the wheels must come off, in which case the relationship or marriage too will fail. So if you wish to find the ideal female partner, it is imperative for you as the male to ascertain what your true purpose in this lifetime is. Only in this way can you attract and find a female who can honestly support your purpose, and aid you in the fulfilment of your fate.

Nevertheless, it is often the case that the female can sense the true purpose of the male, even before he himself is fully aware of what that purpose encompasses. This is especially true when a man marries at a young age. But, although such a man may have found himself the right wife, or rather, although his right wife has found him, unless he starts to fulfil his fate by materialising his true purpose, the marriage will still have a tendency to fail. This is necessarily so, because every female knows within her heart of hearts that she can only fulfil her own fate through the materialisation of the male's purpose. So unless the male is making every effort to materialise his purpose and to fulfil his fate, his spouse will in time become frustrated, and if he still does nothing about correcting the situation, she may even decide to divorce him. Alternatively the female, in her efforts to save the marriage, will start to assume the male role, in the unconscious hope of being able to fulfil her fate. But such a reversal of roles inevitably ends up in the typical "mother and little boy" scenario, in which the woman is constantly displeased with everything and everyone, including her husband!

Another factor to consider is that no man is an island, and consequently, every male normally has at least several other men in his life whose fates are tied in with his own. Such men can be his own son or sons, his brothers, other family members, or colleagues in the workplace. This does not mean that these men do not have individual fates of their own, but that the fates of these men are somehow dependent upon the fate of the male concerned. For example, if you have a son, then unless you fulfil your fate impeccably, you will fail in your duty towards your son. To understand this, realise that your son chose you for a father because of what he needs to learn from your fate, in order to be able to fulfil his own fate. So if you do not fulfil your own fate, your son cannot learn from you what he needs to learn, and in this respect you will fail towards him, irrespective of how good a father you may believe yourself to be. Similarly, if you are the director of a company, but you fail to materialise your full purpose within the business world, all of your male employees will also be hampered in the full development of their own potential for as long as they work for you!

Therefore in relation to everything we have looked at here, it should now be clear why the admonishment to every boy is, "Think, my boy! Think!" In other words, think about the implications of what it is to be male. Think about your purpose. And think about the meaning of either fulfilling or of not fulfilling your fate. But remember that to think means to listen to your heart, and thereby to access and to tap the power of the void, which, in the final analysis, means being truly creative in the materialisation of your purpose and the fulfilment of your fate.

CHAPTER TEN

MYTH ~~TWO~~ Five

MEN SMOKE AND DRINK

THIS IS A MYTH which most definitely cannot be taken at face value, for it can so very easily be misconstrued to mean that it gives the male a license to commit all sorts of atrocities. The real meaning of this myth is that the male must enjoy life to the full. Here again, "What do we mean by the term 'enjoy'?"

Enjoying life does not mean leading a life of debauchery and indulgence. On the contrary, it means that the male must set the example that life is not a sin, but a priceless opportunity – our only opportunity – to learn and to evolve our awareness through experience. But of course, in order to do so, we need to have self-discipline, for we all know only too well how off-putting a bar full of drunken men is. Just take a look at the word "motherless." The implication in this word is that some men are nothing but little boys, and without the discipline imposed by mother, they do not have enough self-discipline to control their indulgences and, as a result, will become motherlessly drunk!

Therefore the ability to enjoy life to the full implies that the male has the necessary self-discipline to show that if we are ever going to manifest our full potential and awareness upon the physical plane, we cannot afford to walk a path of denial. There is no way that we can develop our full potential when we have gaps in our knowledge, and denying ourselves experience does lead to gaps. However, proper care should be taken to understand the difference between denial and restraint, for when this difference is not grasped, it becomes easy to assume that the male has been given a license to act unimpeccably. So let us look at this concept in depth, for unless we grasp it fully, we will indeed be living a life of sin – the sin of not developing our full potential, and thereby not fulfilling our fate.

If we look at everything we have been considering up to this point, it should not be all that difficult to understand that to live life to the full, and to develop our full potential, does not mean that we must indulge in practices which we already know are not life-supportive. For example, how can I justify that stealing from another person is being life-supportive? If I am so badly in need of food, or money, or whatever, then clearly I am badly in need of finding a way in which to support myself and my family. But to steal that food or money from someone else is to rob that person of his livelihood. Likewise, how can I justify murdering another person? If I lack knowledge of what it is to murder, I still cannot justify my actions when I can see for a fact that I will be denying that person his own life and his own opportunity to gain knowledge. How can I impose my will upon that person by saying that I need to know what it is to murder someone, and that that person needs to know what it is to be murdered?

People insist upon making things as complicated as possible, simply so that they can justify their actions in some way. But, none of us have the right to step over the bounds of common sense. Therefore, if you honestly feel a huge need to know what it feels like to stick your hand in a fire, and wish to argue this on the grounds that you cannot deny yourself the experience, then go right ahead and do it. But a far more sensible approach would be to put your hand very close to the fire, in which case you will experience the heat and the pain without having to destroy your hand in the process of learning. In this way you are not denying yourself the experience, but you also have enough self-discipline to exercise restraint. Likewise, if you insist that you need to know what it is to murder another person, then if you have the guts to do so, by all means try! But I can assure you, the moment you look into the eyes of your victim, you will already know what it is to murder without having to kill that person. If, on the other hand, you find yourself being able to kill without flinching, you will know beyond any shadow of doubt that you are a murderer that does not deserve to live!

Living life to the full by not walking a path of denial has nothing at all to do with justifying wrong action. However, in order for us to manifest our full potential upon the physical plane, we need to partake in all of the many richnesses life brings us, whilst standing free and detached from those experiences. In other words, if you enjoy drinking, there is nothing wrong with having a few drinks when you feel like it. But to get drunk is an altogether different kettle of fish. We all know when we have had enough to drink, yet if we don't know when to stop, how much do we really know about our behaviour, and how much self-discipline do we have? If, on the other hand, you do not deny yourself the experience of alcohol, and you learn to drink with self-discipline, you will discover a great deal about your behaviour and about alcohol. But if you simply indulge in drinking, you will discover nothing, and the experience will be a non-experience that still marks a gap in your knowledge.

Exactly the same is true of smoking, or any other so-called vice or sin. If you enjoy smoking, then by all means smoke, as long as you do not smoke to the detriment of your health or, for that matter, to the detriment of anyone else's health! The point is that although we are allowed to and, indeed, must enjoy ourselves upon the physical plane, we must at the same time not become enmeshed by materialism. This is because it is not the physical plane as such that is important, but rather the knowledge gained from life upon the physical plane.

This is a subtle difference which can so easily be overlooked, especially since it is something that requires considerable skill in execution, and therefore also a great deal of self-discipline. We need experience upon the physical plane, and therefore to deny ourselves our experience is every bit as stupid as indulging in it. We are trying to learn. We are not trying to avoid learning, or to become enmeshed in the learning. In this respect, realise that denial is very much a form of self-punishment, and that indulgence demonstrates a lack of self-respect. However, denial and indulgence are but the two sides of the same coin, whilst discipline is the act of treating oneself with respect.

If we consider the term "respect," we discover that it means "to look again," implying the willingness to learn and thereby to uplift oneself. So ask yourself, "Am I willing to learn and to uplift myself? Do I have self-discipline? Do I have self-respect?"

When we look around us today, it is truly frightening and sad to see how many people have given in to indulgences of every description. There are those who indulge in alcohol, or drugs, or even food. There are those who indulge in a fanaticism about health, diets and excessive physical exercise. There are those who indulge in all sorts of strange and abnormal sexual pursuits, and those who indulge in an enforced celibacy. There are those who indulge in work, and who therefore become complete workaholics, as opposed to those who indulge in their sense of laziness and who are therefore always too tired to do an honest day's work. And so the list goes on and on, and yet all of these people are merely denying themselves the opportunity to learn from their experiences, and then to move on.

But by far the saddest form of indulgence is that practised by the great many people who indulge in their sense of unworthiness, and who thereby deny themselves true learning, growth, success, freedom and happiness. Why? Because somewhere along the line, in the process of learning, these people have done something, or experienced something, which they believe has made them unworthy. In other words, we are back to the concept of sin. Having "sinned" in some way, these people are still punishing themselves for knowledge gained, even though they are mostly unconscious of what they are really doing to themselves.

How can knowledge gained possibly be a sin? But here we can so clearly see the huge and powerful influence of social conditioning. If any one person steps out of line in his or her learning, that person is immediately frowned upon as being bad, unworthy, evil or, in short, sinful. Yet, if we cannot have gaps in our knowledge, how can any of us judge another person as being unworthy? We are perfectly within our rights to frown upon that person's behaviour, and to judge that person's experience in terms of being a bad experience, and even to condemn the knowledge gained as being forbidden fruit. But who gives us the right to judge or to condemn the person? No! We are not at liberty to judge another, nor do we have the right to condemn that person. Moreover, we cannot order another to unlearn what they have learned, and in this respect we cannot deny them their experiences! However, we do have the right to restrain a person from indulgent behaviour that is not in any way life-supportive.

To clarify this vital point I would like to work through a few examples of behaviour that is so very prevalent in the world today, and that is causing so many people to feel immoral and unworthy. Let us first of all look at drug abuse.

Being able to stand on our own feet and make our own decisions, based upon our own values, brings tremendous freedom, a freedom that also allows us to participate openly and freely within all of the richnesses of life. By richnesses I am not only referring to the positive, but also to the negative. If we did not have day and night, we would never know the true nature of light, and if we did not have happiness and unhappiness we would never know the true depth of happiness. Likewise, we have to experience all aspects of life upon the physical plane if we are to grasp the real significance of life.

This does not mean that you must become a drug addict in order to know what it is to be free from drugs, but it does mean that if you are not to have gaps in your knowledge, then if drugs surface in your life, you cannot afford to deny yourself the opportunity to learn about them. In other words, if you have never been in contact with drugs in some way, your frame of reference is limited in that area, and so too will be your understanding of life relative to drugs.

If you already know all about drugs, and that they are not for you, then there is no need for you to take drugs. But realise that there are a great many people who have at some time in their lives experimented with drugs, and who may at the time have even believed that it was enjoyable. Now, through having had that experience, rather than spending the rest of their lives fantasising about "tripping out," they have come to the realisation that drugs and "tripping out" are not for them in the long run. Yet such an experience does not make these people drug addicts, and neither does it make them bad people. Such people can only be looked upon as exhibiting evil behaviour when they become enmeshed in indulgence and thereby destroy their own lives, as well as the lives of those around them.

I have used this example, not to make light of the problem surrounding drug abuse, but simply to point out that people are not bad just because of the knowledge they have gained. The problem surrounding drug abuse is huge indeed, but we are not going to resolve it by making people feel inferior or unworthy, or useless. This is especially true of many other problems in the world today which society looks upon as being even more evil than drugs, and which it therefore tries to suppress rather than address.

However, suppression is quite the worst form of indulgence. Whenever we suppress something, either in ourselves, or in someone else, we start to get what I term "the pressure-cooker effect." If you do not allow the steam to escape from a pressure-cooker, the pressure inside eventually becomes so great that the cooker explodes. Exactly the same happens in people. Therefore if a person suppresses a tendency, rather than addressing it, that tendency will eventually explode outwards, with the result that the person concerned will temporarily indulge in that tendency to the limits, and always in the worst possible way. Yet, the very reason why the person tried to suppress the tendency in the first place, is because he already believed that it was bad. So when he explodes, and indulges so horribly in that tendency, such a person finds it exceedingly difficult to forgive himself afterwards. The result is that the man will live a miserable life thereafter, continuing to suppress that which he feels is bad in him, and punishing himself over and over for his sin by not wanting to believe he is worthy of life and of happiness.

Another example that we can look at concerns a great number of heterosexual men who have at some stage in their lives had homosexual experiences in their journey of discovering the meaning of sexuality. But, even if these people enjoyed them, such experiences do not make them homosexual. On the contrary, provided the experience has not made them feel bad about themselves, these men end up being far more secure in their sexuality than they were before. To understand this, we must acknowledge that these people would not have exposed themselves to this type of experience had they been secure in their sexuality in the first place. But now, as a result of their homosexual experiences, they know beyond any shadow of a doubt that they are truly heterosexual.

So often people will end up feeling really terrible about themselves, because they have had certain experiences. Yet this is invariably the result of having tried to suppress their desire for knowledge in the first place. Nevertheless, this is not an easy issue to address, in spite of the examples I have given so far. Therefore let us look at an issue which is even more difficult to handle, and one which is causing a great deal of concern today, namely, child abuse.

Let us say that a man called Joe feels he is somehow attracted by the idea of having sexual intercourse with a child. What is Joe to do? If he merely tries to suppress that urge, he will without doubt either start to fiddle with every child who comes near him, or he will end up raping a child, or perhaps even several children.

In order to grasp Joe's challenge, we need to consider what is actually going on here. First of all, we must remember that there are many people who have been seriously ill at some stage in their lives, but who are now fit and healthy. Therefore just because Joe has this desire now, does not make him an evil man, anymore than a man who has bronchitis is evil. So we can say that Joe's behaviour is not normal, and that he is ill in some way. But this does not mean that Joe cannot be restrained and cured! If, on the other hand, Joe does not want to be cured, or does not want to cure himself, then that is another story! In that case we would have someone on our hands who is wilfully and maliciously wanting to impose his will upon others, with behaviour that is most certainly not life-supportive. We would then have no option other than to confine that person in such a way that he cannot inflict harm upon others. But let us assume that Joe does want to be normal, and wishes to be healed. So the question now is, "How should Joe proceed in trying to heal himself?"

The first thing Joe needs to do, is to realise that his challenge lies in the fact that he has an imbalance of sorts, that is, he is quite literally unbalanced in his sexuality. But whenever we have an imbalance of sorts, irrespective of whether this is a physical imbalance, an emotional imbalance, or a mental imbalance, we invariably manifest some sort of dis-ease. Dis-ease means that we are not at ease with our physical body, our emotions, or our mind, but in every case it is a lack of knowledge in some area of our lives that is bringing about that imbalance and the consequent dis-ease.

In time the dis-ease can become so intense that it begins to cause undue stress upon our being. If the dis-ease is physical we can become physically ill, unless we strive to alleviate the stress. Exactly the same is true of our emotional and mental states of being if we do not strive to alleviate the build-up of emotional or mental stress that results from emotional or mental dis-ease. It is for this reason that people will often resort to smoking, to alcohol, or to drugs, in the same way that someone suffering from physical dis-ease will resort to the use of medication.

Dis-ease does not necessarily mean that a person is ill, but unless the cause of that dis-ease is eradicated, some form of illness will be the end result. But, as we have already noted, all dis-ease is the result of imbalance, and any imbalance is caused by a lack of knowledge. However, since all true knowledge can only be gained through experience, imbalances can only be corrected through the judicious acquisition of experience in that particular area of our lives in which we lack the required knowledge.

I say "judicious," because just as medication should be administered judiciously, so too must we in these cases be prudent in our acquisition of the knowledge we lack. In other words, just as an overdose of painkillers can kill the patient, so too can an over-indulgence in alcohol lead to alcoholism. Similarly, although many men and women have cured themselves of their insecurity regarding their sexuality by allowing themselves homosexual experiences, so have many others succumbed to homosexuality because they abandoned themselves to the experience, rather than having been judicious. Remember that we are here referring to the correction of an imbalance, and not to the normal acquisition of knowledge. In normal life we can never have too much knowledge, but in correcting an imbalance it is perfectly possible to overdose oneself.

This is all very well, but am I advocating that Joe should correct this imbalance within himself by violating the rights of children? No! If you choose to experiment with drugs, you will be doing this only to yourself. Likewise, should you choose to experiment with homosexuality, and do so with another consenting adult man, then that is one thing, but to inflict sexual experimentation upon a child is altogether not on!

But what must Joe do? It is really impossible in a book like this for me to give a detailed approach, for the reason that a hundred men with the same problem will manifest this imbalance in a hundred different ways. Therefore, if the guidance given is to be truly effective, each of those men would have to be given individual guidance and counselling. But since this is not possible here, the best I can do is to give only a very broad perspective that will be common to anyone who has either this or some similar problem.

In many ways this challenge is much the same as the example I gave of putting one's hand in the fire, in order to experience the effects of heat and burns. Drawing from that example, Joe can either put his hand in the fire and burn himself, meaning that he can molest a child sexually and damage himself and the child for life, or he can choose to exercise restraint in the process of learning to correct his imbalance. But it stands to reason that the only viable choice for Joe is to exercise restraint, and the way in which to do this is to start by cultivating self-discipline.

Here it is important to remember that not only does self-discipline lead to self-respect, but that self-discipline also implies being a disciple of the self. In other words, if Joe wants to heal himself, he must become a disciple of his true self, and not a slave to his imbalance. So, the easiest way forward, is for Joe to constantly re-spect himself, his motives, his emotions, his feelings and his thoughts, and to ask himself, "What am I really on about? And what do I really want for myself?" This means that it is imperative for Joe to get to know himself inside out, for only in this way will he be able to work out what turns him on with respect to children, since this is the knowledge he lacks, and it is therefore in this knowledge that lies the key to his healing.

However, if Joe is to get to know himself in this way, he cannot deny himself interaction with children. Only by exposing himself as much as possible to the emotions, the feelings and the thoughts that come up as a result of interacting with children, can Joe begin to establish which particular reactions within himself lead to sexual arousal. At the same time, Joe is also going to have to be hyper-alert, and constantly working at his self-discipline, so that he will be able to restrain himself. But if Joe is willing to do this, then his experiences, harmless as they are because of his self-imposed restraint, will lead him into a greater and greater self-respect, a greater and greater looking at the self, and therefore also into a growing understanding of what lies at the root of his challenge.

Once the cause of the problem has been established, the symptom tends to vanish more or less of its own accord. For example, if you find that you are constantly thirsty because you eat far too much salt, then it is simplicity itself to correct that imbalance just by eating less salt. Likewise, should Joe, for example, find that his problem arises from the fact that he becomes sexually aroused as a result of wanting to dominate a helpless partner sexually, then the chances are that if he continues to re-spect himself he will soon discover that his real problem lies in the fact that he feels sexually inadequate. Once Joe starts to confront his fear of sexual inadequacy with a consenting adult, he will quickly enough start to overcome that fear, and, in so doing, will lose his sexual fascination with children.

Having gained this perspective on the importance and the role of knowledge in our lives, we are in a better position to grasp why, at the beginning of this chapter, I stated that it is the male who must show through example that life is not a sin. Why the male? Why sin? These are two questions which are not at all easy to answer in just a few short sentences. Yet if you carefully consider everything we have learned up to this point, it should not be too difficult to get at least a feeling for what is implied here.

Every male, being a representative of the spirit, has the duty to manifest his full potential upon the physical plane by mapping out the unknown and, in so doing, to play a meaningful role within the evolution of awareness. This means that we cannot afford to have gaps in our knowledge, for not only will those gaps act as handicaps, but they will also cause in us an imbalance of sorts. Needless to say, if we are handicapped and imbalanced we will not be able either to fulfil our full potential, or to evolve awareness in any meaningful way. Therefore it is of the utmost importance that we partake fully in all of the richnesses of life, but without indulging in those experiences.

In this respect, realise that it is not life that is bad or sinful, and neither are our experiences in life bad or sinful. What makes our experiences good or bad is what we do with them, and what makes our lives wholesome or debauched, is our detachment or our indulgence respectively. We are all entitled to enjoy our lives and our experiences, provided that we keep the necessary detachment, in order to maintain self-discipline and retain our self-respect. In fact, it is only by enjoying our lives to the full, but with restraint, that we can bring out our full potential and thereby truly fulfil our fate.

CHAPTER ELEVEN

MYTH SIX
MEN ARE STRONG

THE HIDDEN MEANING within this myth is that the male must anchor the female, irrespective of whether this is the woman in his life, or that greater female, the world around him. It is this tenet that causes most men the greatest amount of confusion nowadays, for it is very rare indeed today to find a man who has been taught this skill, even though this is one of the most important functions of the male.

To anchor means to render the unknown usable upon the physical plane. This means that the male must not only map out the unknown, but make it practical. If we look at the Wright brothers as an example, it is clear to see what is meant by this.

Until the Wright brothers came along, aeroplanes and air travel were impossible. All that was known up until then was that it was not possible to fly a machine heavier than air. But that was the known. The Wright brothers, on the other hand, believing that it was possible to fly, were prepared to enter the unknown, to search there for a way that would enable them to fly. Having found within the unknown certain feelings that seemed to indicate that it was indeed possible, the two brothers were willing to follow their gut feel for the next eleven years, and to explore those feelings in terms of building some sort of a craft. Then, by accessing and drawing upon the power of the void, these two men started to materialise something from out of no-thing. Approximately nine months later they flew just over eight hundred and fifty feet. Two years later they flew for twenty-four miles. Three years after that, they were manufacturing aircraft for the United States army. Air travel had become a reality, and yet another portion of the unknown had become incorporated into the known by two men who were willing, not only to map out that part of the unknown, but also to materialise it.

This is what is meant by anchoring, for the fact is that although a great many people have conceived excellent ideas, until such ideas are anchored upon the physical plane, they remain just that, ideas or, more precisely, pies in the sky! And just like any hot-air balloon that is not anchored, unanchored ideas too float off into nowhere!

However, to anchor upon the physical plane implies the act of intelligent co-operation between, firstly, the sexes; and secondly, the male and his own inner female. But this is where the confusion sets in, for men do not generally know how to access their inner female, let alone how to co-operate with her.

Since the female is the unknown, this should not be all that surprising. Nevertheless, it was only because the Wright brothers could and did enter the unknown, that air travel became a possibility. This process of intelligent co-operation is therefore clearly a most important issue, and in order to grasp it fully, let us take a closer look at it.

We know that the male represents the known and that, relative to him, the female is the unknown. However, if we remain stuck only in the known, this means that the evolution of awareness cannot proceed beyond that point – the best we can do is to keep on reproducing the known in various different forms, but each of those forms, new as they are, offer nothing new in terms of the evolution of awareness. This is the ultimate form of homosexuality, for just as one man cannot impregnate another man, so too is it impossible for the masculine spirit to impregnate the masculine known. So, if the male is to become creative, he must enter the unknown, or in other words, he must penetrate his own inner female and, through the act of intelligent co-operation, fertilise her womb with the power of the void.

This is a concept which goes far beyond the scope of this book, for it encompasses that huge complexity of manifestation known as *the secret of gender*. But for our present purposes it is enough to know that if the evolution of awareness is to progress, the male must keep fertilising that greater female termed the unknown. Therefore, what is meant by "mapping out the unknown," is that the male first penetrates the female unknown. Having done this, he invariably discovers some new form that he feels inspired to bring to birth.

Once that form has been sensed, he must "fertilise" the female, that is, the unknown, for without that fertilisation, the form cannot be brought to birth.

Now, just as it is the male who ejaculates the life-giving sperm on the physical level, so too is it he who must "ejaculate" the creative power of the void on both the emotional and mental levels. But what exactly does this mean?

Remember that the void is no-thing. Yet, just because it is no-thing, that is, just because it is not a thing or, more precisely, any-thing, does not mean that it is not. If you recall, I explained the void in terms of It Is. But whenever the power within the void is tapped, or is made to "ejaculate," It Becomes. In this respect, have you never wondered why men speak of "coming" when they ejaculate? However, although it is possible for men merely to "come" in the sense of a meaningless ejaculation, as for example, in a wet dream, or during masturbation, or during the sexual act in which the man wears a condom, this is not possible in terms of the void. The creative power of the void can only be tapped for the purposes of creation, and therefore, whenever this power is tapped, it is never a mere "coming," but always a full "becoming," meaning a creation. In the case of the Wright brothers that becoming was the prototype of what today we know as aircraft.

Just how the male taps the power of the void is far too complex to explain, and also not really all that important, as far as this book is concerned. What is important, is to know that the male can and does tap that power whenever he enters the unknown with the wish to create. This is exactly the same as the sexual act. No man knows how it is that he becomes sexually aroused, how he reaches a climax, or what causes him to ejaculate. He simply does, or he does not! Although medical science has put forward numerous theories about this subject, the medical scientists are still baffled to explain why sometimes it seems impossible to stimulate a man sexually, why sometimes, even when he does have a full erection, he will fail to reach a climax, and why at other times, that same man can become sexually aroused and ejaculate within seconds, without much apparent stimulation at all!

However, the fact is that no male can become aroused or stimulated, much less ejaculate, when his heart is not in the act. But, as we know, the heart is the feeling, and since all feelings are the expression of irrational knowledge, the implication is that whenever there is a flow of irrational knowledge, that knowledge will express itself in terms of the creative urge in the male becoming aroused and stimulated. Therefore, how the male taps the power of the void is not the issue, since it is a simple fact that whenever the male is in touch with his heart, and thus his feelings, he does tap that power as a result of having become "aroused." Once again, we see how very important it is for the male to be in touch with his feelings.

Nevertheless, it is not enough for the creative urge in the male just to become aroused, for once he has become aroused, the male must fertilise the womb of the unknown, if he is going to bring to birth anything at all. As we know, the "sperm" that is required for this purpose is the male essence contained within the void, and that power is quite literally the knowledge of intelligent co-operation, which, in the final analysis, is what constitutes the creative ability of the male. In this respect, we can note that those men who are "infertile," in the sense of being unproductive and uncreative, are "infertile" because they lack knowledge of the art of intelligent co-operation. Although such men, in their frustration, will quite often "rape" those around them, either emotionally or mentally, they never manage to bring to birth that which they desire, for the simple reason that rape is the antithesis of intelligent co-operation. In order to get a better understanding of this, let us look at a simple example.

Say you are my boss at work. Although I am a man, because I am your employee I have to take your lead and support your purpose within the company, and therefore, relative to you, I am female. This is what is known as the relative factor of awareness, a concept which I explained in *This Darned Elusive Happiness*. Now if you want me to develop a new concept for the company, you are going to have to get me, firstly, to conceive your idea; and secondly, to bring that idea to birth in terms of something practical on the physical plane.

However, if you cannot communicate your idea, which will be either because you yourself are not clear about what you want, or simply because you lack communication skills, I will not be able to conceive your idea. If I cannot conceive your idea, or if I just do not want to, whether this is because I hate your guts, or feel threatened by you, I will not bring anything to birth. But whether it is you who cannot "impregnate" me, or whether it is I who refuse to be "impregnated," the bottom line is that it will not help if you now try to force me into bringing something to birth.

Consequently, no matter how much you "rape" me, the end result will not be what you wish for! If you truly want me to bring to birth your "baby," you will have to get me to co-operate with you intelligently. How you do that, will depend upon you as an individual. But the point is that it is up to you as the male to initiate that act of intelligent co-operation!

At this stage, an important issue to take note of is that those men who are "infertile" because they lack knowledge of the art of intelligent co-operation, and who resort to "rape," will often attempt to substitute the creative power of the void in some way. They usually do this by implanting in their victims fear based upon emotional or mental manipulation. This fear can be as gross as the fear of being fired, or it can be as subtle as the fear of falling from grace, and therefore of not being invited to play golf with the boss on Saturday afternoons. Yet realise that although it is possible to bring to birth something out of fear, that is, through "rape," that product will lack inspiration and creativity, for it is quite literally fear-full, and mostly ends up being an "abortion."

I have specifically used this example of an employer and his male employee for two reasons. First of all, to stress the fact that, as opposed to physical gender, which is fixed, male and female are states of awareness that are relative to each other, and thus to remind you that this should never be forgotten in working with the relative factor of awareness. Secondly, to point out that the relative factor of awareness should never be misconstrued as being a justification for homosexuality. In this respect, and especially since homosexuality is today becoming a big issue in the world, it will be worthwhile to digress for a brief overview of this subject.

Although we have seen that the relative factor of awareness is constantly in operation and that as a result men, like women, are forever switching back and forth between the two polarities of awareness, the fact is that we cannot afford not to remain true to our physical gender. The reason for this is that unless we remain true to our gender, we have no hope of being able to unfold our full potential upon the physical plane.

To remain true to one's gender means that the male has to embrace the female fully in the act of intelligent co-operation, for only in this way can he map out the unknown and incorporate it into the known. If he fails to do this, the man concerned remains firmly stuck within the confines of the masculine known. As we noted earlier, unless this situation is corrected, the fact of being confined only to the known must and will begin to cause a gap and therefore an imbalance in that man's knowledge of the feminine unknown. The danger here is that any imbalance causes a distortion in one's perception. Because of that perceptual distortion, the imbalance continues to become worse, in that such a man becomes more and more caught up within the confines of the known. Being caught up in such a way, the man increasingly excludes himself from any meaningful interaction with the unknown through the medium of the female. Slowly but surely such a man begins to lose touch with the true purpose of the male, which is to engage the female in the act of intelligent co-operation so as to map out the unknown, and thereby to incorporate her into his life.

The reasons for the man not including the female fully in his life vary greatly between one individual and another, and even between one culture and another. The extent of the separativeness also varies a great deal. But broadly speaking, it always boils down to the fact that the man concerned elevates the masculine above the feminine. However, by doing so, as paradoxical as this may appear to be, such a man is no longer true to his own gender. By favouring the masculine, he is inadvertently becoming prone to those thought patterns that must ultimately lead to homosexuality. I am not inferring here that every man who is separative in his approach towards life is necessarily going to become homosexual, but the implications of this separativeness are nonetheless clear to see. If such an imbalance is not corrected, but is instead perpetuated lifetime after lifetime, the prejudices which arise from this distorted perception invariably give rise to thought patterns that become more and more biased towards the masculine, until eventually they culminate in a lifetime, or even several lifetimes, of homosexuality.

To elevate one sex above the other is therefore a far cry from remaining true to one's gender and, as we noted earlier, unless we remain true to our gender we cannot possibly unfold our full potential. It is a deep unconscious knowledge of this fact that gives rise to the instinctive tendency in the homosexual man to adopt either the male or the female role in his relationship with another man. And it is this that is behind the fact that when two men are in a romantic relationship, the unspoken command of both men is that one of them must adopt the female role, in their attempts to substitute the normal male-female interaction which enables both the man and the woman to unfold their potential.

The man who adopts the female role is invariably the one who feels the most inadequate about his masculinity. These feelings of inadequacy result from such a man having lost all sense of what the true purpose of the male entails. Therefore, the man feels the need for a male in his life who will provide for him the lead, point out the direction, and prescribe the method to be employed. The irony here lies in the fact that by having favoured masculinity over femininity, such a man has now swung to the opposite polarity of his awareness, and in the process has become more female than a woman, even though he is in a male incarnation! Feeling more female than male, this man is the passive partner, and he can only come into touch with masculinity if his partner plays for him the active male role, but most specifically in the sexual act. Why specifically sexual? Simply because, being a male, no man can ever feel fulfilled at an emotional and a mental level with a male partner. As a result, physical sex in which his is being "fertilised" becomes all-important to the passive man, in spite of the fact that in not being able to conceive, he still always feels somehow "empty," no matter how often he is engaged in sex.

Consequently, the passive man will unconsciously begin to long for fulfilment, but not realising that it is his own masculine potential he longs for, the man inevitably misinterprets this in terms of the physical. Therefore he starts to seek out men who are willing to have sex several times a day, or he seeks out multiple partners and, in some cases, even sadists. For the passive man seeking fulfilment, any physical pain inflicted during the act of sex lasts longer than the act itself, and so, while the pain endures, he feels at least something over and above the gnawing sense of emptiness. It is also for this reason that the passive man is never all that interested in a man unless that man is hung like a stallion, and why he will also not shy away from the opportunity to be "gang-raped" by a group of men.

The active partner, on the other hand, also cannot find fulfilment other than a temporary sexual satisfaction. Although this man is normally much more in touch with his masculinity than the passive man, he can still sense that his relationship is fruitless. No matter how much he may enjoy the sexual act, at a deep level he knows that just as his partner can never fall pregnant, so too can his partner never call forth in him the creative power of the void. As a result, the active man feels impotent and uncreative, and because of that, he begins to become inwardly frustrated. At first such a man can alleviate the frustration to some extent by having multiple partners, but the relief found is short-lived. As the frustration continues to build, the man will eventually turn to either sadism or bisexuality for relief. If he goes the sadistic route, he normally becomes ever more brutal during the sexual act, until finally he is incapable of climaxing unless he can inflict severe pain. If, on the other hand, he becomes bisexual, he invariably loses himself in promiscuity, including "swinging" with married couples, an act which gives him the opportunity to take sadistic pleasure in having sex with another man's wife while the man watches.

Although I know that many gay men will wish to shout me down furiously for what I have stated here, none of them can deny the validity of the bottom line. The fact remains that, as men, they can never fulfil their masculine potential, and neither can they evolve their awareness in any meaningful way whilst they remain caught up in homosexuality, irrespective of whether they practise it or not. Even gay couples who have been together faithfully and "happily" for many years, and who have never allowed themselves to engage in the type of behaviour patterns described above, cannot deny that somewhere deep down inside they are unhappy because they feel unfulfilled, no matter how much they may want to argue this point.

Furthermore, I wish to stress that I personally do not sit in judgement of homosexuals. The self-inflicted emotional pain and cruelty found in the world of the homosexual is no worse than that found amongst heterosexuals, for it is in truth only the form that differs. Yet, each and every one of us must find our way by ourselves, and learn to stand strong and firm in our own knowledge. What I have stated here is objective fact, and nothing more. To illustrate this, I am not frightened to admit that I too have had homosexual experience. Because the only knowledge is that which we have gained through experience, how can I be exempt? So I speak from personal experience, and not from hearsay or from thumb-sucking. I have had to learn the hard way, and although I do not regret the experience, because of the knowledge I have gained, homosexuality is nevertheless a learning curve I do not yearn to repeat!

If you are homosexual, know that I do not condemn you in any way, but if you are wanting to claim you power as a male, then you will have to reconsider your behaviour and sexual preferences very seriously in the light of what I am revealing in this book. Admittedly in this brief overview of homosexuality I have left far too many questions unanswered. But for the purposes of this book, it is enough to allow us to see homosexuality in context with the quest for maleness. Accordingly I am endeavouring only to point the gay reader in the right direction. More than this I cannot do here, for the simple reason that the subject is extremely complex, and cannot be dealt with adequately in a few short paragraphs.

However, one final point still needs to be addressed, and this is the question, "Is it true that some men are born homosexual?" From what we have seen so far, the answer is, "No! There are no accidents at birth!" All men are born as males with a masculine potential which it is their duty to unfold. We make ourselves into whatever we want to, partly through our social conditioning, partly through our self-image and partly through our innermost desire to learn. However, if you consider yourself to have been homosexual from the day you were born, then this is only in the sense that many lifetimes of imbalance have finally caught up with you. This is exactly the same as the way in which many lifetimes of imbalance can cause a person to be born a cripple, or even mentally retarded. The bottom line being that any imbalance must, and will, eventually manifest itself on the physical plane, and thus in the life of the person concerned, irrespective of whether this happens to be in a mental, physical or emotional form, or even in what could be looked upon as forming a part of one's genetic make-up. If, on the other hand, you do not feel that you were born homosexual, but you just feel the need to explore your sexuality through the medium of homosexuality, then bear in mind that although none of us can have gaps in our knowledge, this does not mean that in order to fill such gaps we must become entrapped in them. It is perfectly possible to learn and to move on, irrespective of whether you were "born" homosexual or whether you are merely experimenting. But the problem with most people is that they like to indulge in the experience, rather than treating it as a learning curve which brings not only a gift of knowledge, but also the keys to liberation from that challenge.

Returning now to the concept of intelligent co-operation, you will find that the best way of learning this skill is to start co-operating with the outer females in your life, irrespective of whether these are your spouse, a male employee, your son, who, if he is still at home, will also be female relative to you, or just the world at large. By studying these outer females, and seeing how we relate to them, and they to us, we also learn how to differentiate between the two polarities of male and female within our own awareness. In other words, we begin to see when we ourselves are either in male mode, or in female mode, and how these two modes can be made to complement each other in the act of intelligent co-operation.

By studying the female in others, and by learning to recognise the female mode in ourselves, we are in effect learning how to co-operate with our own inner female. In practical terms this means that we begin to learn how the rational mind and the irrational feelings arising from the heart complement each other, and can therefore be made to work together. Naturally, the easiest place to start is with the woman in your life. To make this clear, let us once again look at an example.

How often does a man not say one thing, based upon what is for him the known, only to find that his wife will express a feeling that seems to contradict his view? When this happens, it does not mean that one is right and the other is wrong. On the contrary, this means that the man is being given the opportunity to become creative, since his wife has stimulated in him a flow of irrational knowledge.

If the man simply snubs his wife, he casts aside this opportunity and, in doing so, fails to become "aroused." If, on the other hand, he accepts the stimulation offered by his wife, he will begin to explore the unknown she is bringing him and, as a result, irrational knowledge will begin to flow. The secret here lies in the male's willingness to say, "How can I use what I already know, coupled with this bit of the unknown my wife brings me, to achieve my desired goal?" To do this, the male must penetrate his own inner female, that is, the unknown within, and allow his feelings to guide him into the act of intelligent co-operation between mind and heart. But, as we already know, that act of intelligent co-operation is the fertilisation of the female womb, and once fertilisation has taken place, a birth of sorts will be the result.

So if you wish to claim your full potential as a male, you cannot avoid learning to co-operate intelligently with the females in your life. Learn to listen to them, instead of merely hearing them. Learn not to fob them off, but instead to respect them, but most especially in the sense of re-spect, that is, looking again and again at what it is they are telling you or showing you in whatever way. If you do this, you will find yourself automatically beginning to co-operate intelligently with every female, and with no more thinking involved than when you find yourself having become sexually aroused and highly excited by a sexy young lady!

No man can will himself into having an erection, and neither can any man will himself into "coming." To become creative the male needs to be stimulated by the presence of the unknown, and once he penetrates that unknown, the flow of irrational knowledge will cause him to "climax" in the formation of some-thing new. Having climaxed, he has in effect called forth the creative power of the void, and through that act has fertilised the womb of the feminine unknown. After that the birth is inevitable, and the male will anchor upon the physical plane some aspect of the unknown that has not been in existence before.

This then leads us into the next myth, because in order for the male to anchor the unknown upon the physical plane, he must not only be able to initiate the act of intelligent co-operation, but he must also know how to contain the female, if he is not to become lost in the chaos and disorder of the unknown.

CHAPTER TWELVE

MYTH SEVEN
MEN MUST BE SUCCESSFUL

FROM WHAT WE have already noted in the last chapter, the real meaning of being successful is that the male must be practical, if he is not to become enmeshed and lost within the chaos of the unknown. In relation to this, remember that the sole purpose of life upon the physical plane is to materialise our full potential within physical life. But, in order to do so, we must be practical – untested ideas floating around in the mind, and unfulfilled dreams, are more than useless.

True knowledge can only arise out of practical experience, and so it is not airy-fairy thinking that is called for, but action! However, action which does not go anywhere, or which does not yield some sort of dividend, is stupid and useless. Therefore all our actions must be practical, in that they must yield fruit of some sort. In other words, we must have proof upon the physical plane that knowledge is indeed power. This is simply because "knowledge" which does not yield fruit is not real knowledge, and neither can it be termed power.

Consequently, we need to learn to differentiate between all of our life's experiences. Although all experience yields knowledge, realise that we can only make use of that knowledge if we claim it in terms of power, and power is dependent upon our needs in the moment. In order to grasp this, think of a student at university who is studying law. Now, if that student wants to become a lawyer, his needs are to study everything related to law. In the process he will gain a lot more knowledge than just that which pertains to law, and this is fine and good, for he will graduate as well-educated and highly proficient. But it will not benefit that student to lose focus in his studies and to study physics and chemistry, medicine and religion, architecture and engineering, all in the name of becoming a lawyer. If any student does this, he will normally end up failing law! Each of these disciplines are specialised pursuits, and it is simply not possible to do so many degrees simultaneously. But even if it were possible, such a student will still end up having lost sight of why he wanted to study law in the first place!

Life, and what we need to learn in life, is exactly the same. We each have a specific purpose to fulfil, and in relation to this we must remain focussed on our fate. To do so, the male needs to learn to contain the female, meaning that he must learn how to navigate his way within the unknown, in pursuit of the knowledge he needs, in order to fulfil his purpose. In this respect, it is also very much up to the male, not only to provide the female in his life with the correct lead, but also to point out to her the direction to be followed, and the method to be employed in mapping out the unknown.

This is important, because the female is by her very nature chaotic, since being the tonal, which is every-thing, she more often than not thinks one thing whilst feeling another. As a result, it is perfectly normal for the female to be busy with several things at the same time, whilst also being perfectly capable of finding order within disorder, and logic in the irrational. From an objective point of view it may appear that the female's life is a disorderly chaos, but within that mixture of the known and the unknown, the partially-completed tasks amidst several new projects, the mixture of clear thoughts and only vaguely sensed feelings, the female knows exactly where she is and where she is going.

Therefore every female has the ability to talk to a friend on the telephone whilst cooking breakfast, seeing to it that Johnny brushes his teeth before going to school, reminding her husband that his great aunt is coming to dinner that evening and that he must not forget that she likes her gin and bitters at six-thirty sharp, that he must not wear jeans, which his aunt detests, and that he must remember to fetch Johnny from his soccer match on the way home. In between all of this, it is also not uncommon that the female will also rescue the parrot from its fight with the dog, remember to feed the parrot and the cat, phone Johnny's school to find out if Johnny really did not have any homework the day before, and make a mental note that on Friday evening she and her husband have to attend the birthday party of a friend who has asked her to bring special perrier water stocked at that odd little shop just two blocks from the library off Markson Street, where parking can be found up the alleyway behind the supermarket at which she can also buy Johnny a new pair of soccer shorts, for it is so much cheaper there, and, oh yes, then she can at the same time drop off her books at the library! All that activity, planning, thinking, and recollecting within the space of breakfast-time, whilst also doing her make-up, drying her hair, and getting suitably dressed for a cold day that could become warmer later on whilst she is in town where it could become difficult to find somewhere to take off her vest!

It might look like a total chaos, but for the female, this is order within disorder, and logic within what, for the male, is more akin to mental gymnastics that seem to be highly irrational! Yet realise that until such time as a man begins to claim his power as a male, he will often end up indulging in this type of female chaos, and, as a result, will vacillate between being a nutty professor and a dithering and doubting old hen who is not too sure what she (he) is clucking about! Whilst this state of being is completely natural for the female, it spells disaster for the male.

The female, being the unknown, is dependent upon the male to contain her. If she is not being contained this state of being will either force her into going over the top, or else it will cause her to start feeling inadequate and somehow inferior. Therefore, unless the male is capable of containing the female, he will not only have a terrible relationship with females, but most important of all, he will also have a terrible relationship with his own inner female, who in not being contained, will be turning him into a nutty professor or an old hen!

Once again, the easiest way in which to grasp this, is to look at the woman in your life. Being contained does not mean that the female is being suppressed or dominated in any way. Instead it means that the male has absorbed her fully into his life, in such a way that she feels acknowledged, loved and cared for. If the male does this, he automatically values her opinions and feelings with respect to all of their mutual endeavours and will always take them fully into account. By acknowledging, loving, caring for, and so, fully absorbing the female into his life, the male makes sure that the female is always included in all of his decisions and plans. Consequently, the female does not have to worry about where they are going, or whether they have enough finances for the bond on the house, or whether the insurance premiums are up to date, for she knows her male's strategy and plans as the provider, and therefore knows that he is seeing to all of that. Being freed in this way, she can now concern herself with the needs of the moment, irrespective of whether this means having to rescue the parrot, phone the school, organise dinner, or remind her husband to fetch Johnny after soccer.

The result of this intelligent co-operation between male and female is that the female has the freedom, not only to cope with the needs of the moment, but also to go into the unknown, and there to search her own feelings in connection with the male's quest for clarity. Knowing that she does not have to worry about hunting and providing as such, for that is the male's responsibility, the female can instead concentrate on how best to guide him in achieving the clarity he seeks. This she does, not because she is clairvoyant, but simply because she is so highly skilled in doing multiple tasks simultaneously, that she can and does sense the interrelationship of everything. In fact, it is exactly because of her ability to sense the interrelationship of all, that she can and does manage to do so many things at once. Yet, this ability is very much a sensing rather than a knowing, and so, the true female can seldom explain to the male why she feels something in a certain way. Such feelings she will simply dump in his lap, and it will then be up to him to figure out what those feelings translate into, and what best to do with the facts uncovered in this way. This is part and parcel of what is meant by containing the female. But in order to gain a better understanding of this, let us look at an example I used in *Unveil the Mysteries of the Female*, but now from the perspective of the male.

Clint has been offered the opportunity to invest in a small printing business, but although he feels drawn to the prospect, he is not comfortable enough to accept the proposal without further consideration. Clint decides to enlist the aid of his wife, Claire, and so, brings the subject up after work that evening. By doing this, Clint is not only using Claire as a mirror of his own inner female, but he is also initiating the act of intelligent co-operation between both his outer and inner female, and himself.

At first Claire does not really know what to think about the proposal, except that she somehow feels it could be a good investment, provided Clint knew more about the practicalities involved in printing. Realising that Claire is right, in that he does not know much about the printing business, Clint sets out the following morning to hunt down as much information as he can about printing.

In the meantime, Claire receives a phone call in the morning, from a friend who tells her about the husband of a friend of hers, who has just started up a business importing paper at bargain prices. Just then Claire hears the parrot screeching from the sewing room and, sensing that his perch has been knocked over, she rushes into the room to find the dog and the parrot in a violent disagreement. Having rescued the parrot, Claire returns to the phone with the vague feeling that the incident with the parrot, the news about imported paper, and the highly indignant dog are all somehow connected to something she should be taking note of.

Later that morning, Claire is preparing to do some shopping for dinner, and remembers that she must also return her library books towards the end of the week. Rather than letting it wait, Claire decides to drop the books off on her way to do the shopping and, at the same time, to see if she can find in the library any books on printing that Clint might find useful.

Claire does not find anything enlightening about printing at the library, but in talking to one of the librarians, the lady suggests that Clint should try to get the information he is seeking from the Chamber of Commerce and Industry. Armed with at least that much information, Claire goes shopping, and then home. Once she is home, she phones Clint to tell him about the librarian's suggestion.

In the meantime, Clint has also been asking around for more information about the printing business, and has found out that unless the printer has access to paper at a reasonable price, it can be a risky business. Having found the direction he should be taking in investigating the proposal, Clint shares this information with Claire when she phones him. Now that the direction has been made clear to her, Claire excitedly tells Clint about the news her friend gave her that morning, and also goes on to tell him about the librarians suggestion. However, after the phone call, Claire, for some strange reason, begins to feel uneasy about something she cannot put her finger on.

Later in the day, while engaged in conversation with Clint's great aunt, Claire tells the aunt about the incident with the parrot and the dog. But the aunt, in her usual offhand manner, dismisses the incident with a wave of her hand. She sarcastically goes on to point out that dogs tend to be just as stupid as their masters, especially when, having knocked someone off his perch, they end up being far too "honourable," because of a misplaced sense of loyalty, to put up a really good fight for their own rights. Once again Claire gets the uneasy feeling that all of this is somehow connected to something she should be taking note of.

However, it is only later, when Clint joins them for drinks, and tells them about his own day, including his trip to the Chamber of Commerce and Industry, that Claire begins to see the thread of meaning in what she had been sensing all day. When he tells them that the only thing he managed to learn from the Chamber of Commerce is that there is fierce competition between printers, Claire suddenly realises that this is what the parrot and the dog had showed her that morning. So it is now clear to her that if Clint is going to make this business work, he will, as his aunt pointed out earlier, have to be prepared to fight for his rights.

Later that evening, once Aunty has gone home, Claire shares her insight with Clint and, in absorbing what Claire noticed, Clint realises that if he is going to make a success of the printing business, he will indeed have to put aside his natural tendency not to want to impose himself upon others, in the sense that he will not be able to afford to worry about knocking others off their perch, as it were. Clint now concludes that the only way he will be able to compete in the printing business, is to use his and Claire's newly-found contacts in the paper industry to undercut other printers, even if this does mean the possibility of putting them out of business.

Whilst both of them have been going about their own roles within daily life, Clint has found the clarity he was seeking, and Claire helped him enormously in this tasks, even though she never once tried to tell her husband what to do, or in any way tried to assume the male role of being the hunter. From this example it should also be clear how the female can and does take the male's lead, in that Claire did not question her husband's interest in the printing business, but instead, busied herself in following the direction he pointed out and, through that, also gave him her full support in his sense of purpose.

Yet realise that Claire was only able to co-operate with Clint in this manner because Clint was being strong and confident in his masculinity and, as a result, also clear in his sense of purpose. If Clint had been insecure in his masculinity, he would have been uncertain and confused as to what to make of the proposal, for in not being able to contain his inner female, he would have been swamped with all kinds of half-formulated thoughts, mixed feelings and, in short, a highly confusing array of indecisions. In that state of confusion he would not have been able to give Claire any real direction and she, in turn, would also have become confused about what Clint was really looking for. Not being contained by her husband, in the sense of not knowing what he was wanting from her, the chances are that Claire would never have been able to figure out any of the indications and guidance she received from the world around her, not because she lacked intelligence, but simply because she had no leadership, no direction and no sense of purpose.

The inevitable question that every man comes up with at this point is, "But how do I contain the female?" I know that it all seems to be very confusing, but it is also in this apparent confusion where lies the answer. Whenever a man becomes confused, it is precisely because he has walked into the fatal trap of fusing together the male and the female within himself. Although the male needs to incorporate the female within his own state of beingness, he can never afford to do so in a willy-nilly manner. The unknown must be mapped out and brought into the known, but we can only do this piece by piece, and each piece has to be carefully earmarked in the sense that we know exactly what it is we need to bring forth. Simply to grab at a chunk of the unknown is the same as a naive student who goes to university with absolutely no idea of what he is going to study. Yet it is truly frightening to see how many men do just this in their lives. Having no real sense of purpose other than their preconceived ideas about what life owes them, many men spend a great deal of their lives drifting around aimlessly within the unknown, all the while wondering why their lives are such a chaotic mess!

To contain the female means that even if we are not sure what our purpose is, we must at least be sure of that much! How can you be confused about not knowing something? Such an indulgence is ludicrous! You either know something, or you don't. So there is nothing to be confused about. Therefore, if you do not know what your purpose is, then set out in search of it. But this is something we have already looked at earlier in this book, and we do not need to repeat it here.

Let it suffice for me to remind you that you must take stock of everything in your life. By taking stock of everything, you will already be containing your own inner female and, once she is contained, she can assist you in your search instead of confusing you even more! Just remember that you will get nowhere if you keep fusing the male and the female. Each has a specific role to play, and although they should be made to complement each other in the act of intelligent co-operation, the onus is on you as the male to discriminate between being Arthur or Martha.

CHAPTER THIRTEEN

MYTH EIGHT
MEN SHOULD BE MARRIED

THIS MYTH IS NOT particularly esoteric in that its meaning is fairly obvious, and this is that the male must be committed. However, do not fall into the trap of taking this at face value, for it must never be forgotten that the only real commitment there is, is commitment to the self. It is simply not possible to be committed to anyone or anything outside of ourselves, for the simple reason that if we were to try, we would be negating our own freedom.

Therefore the concept of marriage and commitment boils down to the fact that the two people concerned must be committed to their own inner counterpart, of which the outer partner is a mirror. Consequently, when it is stated that the man should be married, it means that he must be committed to his own inner female. Commitment to the female, though, does not necessarily mean that every man must be physically married in the accepted sense of the word. What it means is that there must be an inner marriage or, more precisely, a firm commitment between the male and his own inner female. But the only way of learning what this actually means in practice, is to begin by using all outer females as mirrors.

Because of the tremendous difficulty in seeing ourselves objectively, we all need a physical mirror to show us where the opposite polarity of our awareness is at. Yet I stress again that this does not necessarily imply marriage. The reason I stress this point is to emphasise the relative factor of awareness, which men are all too prone to forget. Therefore a mirror of your own inner female does not necessarily mean only your wife. If your son is being scattered and unfocussed in his schoolwork, or if a male employee is lacking in direction and fritters away valuable time fiddling with irrelevant details, take it as fact that they are mirrors showing you that your own inner female is not being contained!

It is also important to stress that none of us can ever realise our full potential unless we can and do co-operate with the opposite polarity of our own awareness, for to be only one polarity means that we are only half a person. No matter how hard we try, the fact is that there cannot be something like half a male. You are either fully male, or you are an it! Just like a magnet cannot be a magnet if it has only one polarity, so too can there only be a north pole if there is also a south pole. So a male can only be a true male if he is married to his polar opposite, in the sense that he is committed to his own inner female. But in order to have that commitment, the male must also be committed to the mirror of that inner female which, as we know, is the outer female in his life. This, of course, implies everything we have been looking at so far, and which all boils down to the act of intelligent co-operation.

Needless to say, none of us would ever know how to co-operate with our inner counterparts if we did not have the opportunity to learn that co-operation with our physical mirrors. Therefore, by studying the outer females in his life, the male learns how he relates to them, and how they relate to him. In doing so, the male also learns how to differentiate between the two polarities of his own awareness, and how the two can be made to complement each other.

It is always at this point that the million dollar question will surface: "How do I do that?" Unfortunately there is no other way to learn than through personal experience. People always make the mistake of wanting to know everything up front before they put anything into practice, but life does not work that way. If it did, we would all still be waiting to be born! We only find out how something works once we are doing it. And exactly the same is true here. If you want to know how this works, you are just going to have to use the techniques you are being given in this book to guide you into gaining your own experience. That experience will be your knowledge, and once you have knowledge you will find that there is nothing left to understand! We only seek understanding when we do not yet have the knowledge.

The only real guidance I can give you here, is to say that if you want to know what it means to co-operate with your own inner female, then learn what it is to co-operate with the outer females in your life. If you want to know what it is to be a true male, then study your polar opposite, that is, the woman in your life. There is simply no other way. If you want to know what is real peace, then you should study war, for unless you can see the darkness, you will never know the true meaning of light. Likewise you will never understand yourself, unless you study your polar opposite. And you will never grasp your own inner female, unless you study your outer female, for just as you cannot see your own face without a mirror, so too will you never get to know your inner female without an outer mirror.

Although I have already explained the concept of mirrors in several of my other books, it will help if we briefly summarise the salient points here. Firstly, remember that any person who draws our attention in some way, shows us aspects of ourselves. Here it is important to bear in mind that you cannot perceive something that is not within your frame of reference, and if it is within your frame of reference, it means that you know it from your own experience.

Secondly, all the people around you are important. They are in your life for a reason, and this means that their behaviour is showing you something about yourself. Thirdly, look for the bottom line in your mirrors. In other words, do not take what you see in your mirrors at face value. Therefore if you see a colleague at work filching company stationery, but you never steal anything, ask yourself, "But in what way *do* I steal?" Perhaps you are stealing time from your family by spending too much time at work. Perhaps you are stealing another man's wife by having an affair with her. Look for it. You will find it!

Fourthly, remember that our mirrors show us both the positive and the negative behaviour. Look at both as being aspects of yourself. Fifthly, our mirrors can be past, present or future mirrors. Accordingly, when you see somebody's behaviour, you can be sure either that you are doing the same right now and that is why you see it, or that you've done it in the past, or that you recognise it as something you could possibly be guilty of in the future, even though you may not be doing it at the moment.

Finally, always acknowledge that the female shows us aspects of the unknown that we should be concentrating on right now. Therefore, instead of shouting and screaming at your wife that you don't know what she's talking about, take it as fact that what she is trying to draw your attention to, is that aspect of your knowledge which is still lacking. In other words, it's that part of the unknown which should be mapped out and incorporated into the known.

By far the easiest way to get started in the right direction with respect to this, is to begin with your own behaviour. Make a list of all the ways in which you do not use the females in your life as your mirrors, and so do not co-operate with them. With this list, you will be amazed to see how quickly you find that you are becoming incapable of blaming anyone, least of all females. Instead you will come to see that what you are looking at in terms of behaviour in others, is in actual fact only a reflection of your own lack of intelligent co-operation.

Although it may appear as if I have given you very little in this section with which to work, the truth is that I have in fact given you more than you can digest in this lifetime. By telling you to study the females in your life, to see them as mirrors of your own unknown inner counterpart, and then to seek co-operation with them from what you have learned through your study, is the task of a lifetime! What more do you need? I cannot study for you. I cannot learn on your behalf. Only you can study, learn and seek the required co-operation. And if you do, you will no longer need anyone telling you what to do.

For now you may feel as if you do not know where to begin. But that is not important. Life has no beginning and no end, and therefore we can simply start anywhere at any time. Even if you just sit down and admit to yourself that you are at a loss, you are already well on your way to learning. How come? Because probably for the very first time in your life you have come to the honest realisation that you have no clue what it means to be a male, let alone how to seek co-operation with the opposite sex. That in itself is an invaluable realisation, and a very fine state of mind, for unless we come to the point of being able to acknowledge that what we think we know may well be nothing more than a higgledy-piggledy mess of preconceived ideas and prejudices, we remain closed to true learning and to true knowledge.

So do not feel despondent if you feel as if you do not know where to go from here. In not knowing, you have already taken the first step in the right direction – you have opened yourself to finding out, to learning. In being open you cannot help but to learn, and every new insight, every new bit of experience gained, will lead you one step further, and that step in its turn will reveal the next step, and so on. Just start. How you start is not important. And above all, remember that understanding is only for fools who are too lazy to want to learn. Understanding means the ability to grasp information imparted. But it is not information you are needing here. It is knowledge you need, and knowledge can only be gained through practical experience.

Having said that, there is one final word of advice you will find invaluable: allow the female into your life. In trying to discriminate between the known and the unknown, and in trying to keep the focus, men all too often forget that in order to be a whole person they must allow the female in. But unless you are a whole person, how will you ever manage to be fully male?

Therefore when you are desperately trying to concentrate on getting a job done, and your wife insists on chirping in your ear about Johnny's schoolwork, don't tell her to shut up and leave you alone! Put down your work and listen to her. I can assure you, one way or another, she is telling you something that is vital to the work you are busy with! If you are trying your best to remain focussed on what is not working in your marriage, and your daughter keeps waking up at night having wet her bed, don't tell your wife she must take the child to a psychologist. Your daughter is telling you what is wrong in your marriage. Talk to your wife about it. Likewise, if you are trying your best to meet deadlines at work, and one of your male employees keeps arriving late for work, don't fire him. Talk to him and listen to what he is telling you. One way or another, that man will let you know why everything in your company is always behind schedule.

If you are to succeed as a male, you must be willing to allow the female into your life, irrespective of whether this is your wife, your children, your employees, or just the world in general. To allow the female in means that you are willing to listen to her, not so that you can prove her wrong, but in the sense that, because she is your polar opposite, she is showing you the other side of the coin. Always remember that there is no such thing as a coin with only one side. To be anything at all, a coin must have two sides! But more important than anything else, is in fact that by allowing the female in, you will start to listen to your own inner feelings instead of always just listening to your logical reasoning!

CHAPTER FOURTEEN

MYTH NINE
MEN ARE SEXUAL STUDS

WE COME NOW to the final myth, and the one which embodies a principle that is by far the most important of all, namely, that the male creates. In our consideration of this myth we will clearly see how it reveals the ultimate meaning contained in the first myth, and how all the intermediary myths are merely aspects of this one truth. Therefore let us look at what is really entailed in this principle.

The male, being the spirit of man made manifest, creates. This is all very well, but to create is a huge responsibility, for as we know only too well, it is possible to create all sorts of things. Therefore the male can create chaos or order. He can create happiness or unhappiness. He can create war or peace, wealth or poverty, health or illness, evolution or degeneration, empowerment or disempowerment. In short, the male can create forms which uplift life, or he can create monsters that destroy life.

The purpose of the female, on the other hand, is to co-operate intelligently with the male, and to support and to nurture his purpose. Do you see the implications here? Do you begin to discern the vitally important role of the female in the life of the male? So what do you expect from the females in your life? Do you expect them to support and nurture destruction? Or do you expect them to support and nurture that which uplifts? For example, has your wife ever complained to you that you work too hard? If she has, have you become angry at her for not supporting you in your work? Yet realise that by working so hard, your business has swallowed you, and is also destroying you, your marriage, and even your health, your life. Is this what you want your wife to nurture?

At this point, the question that always comes up is, "Why is it not the female who creates?" After all, as so many men have learned from painful experience, anything men can do, women can do even better! Although this is a perfectly good question, it is not one that I can answer! But then, can anyone answer such a question?

Remember that it is not man who made men and women, much less males and females. I am only pointing out what is. I have no power to change that. Neither do you, or anyone else. Yet nothing stops any of us from trying. In this respect every woman is free to try to change the natural order of things, and therefore if she wishes to see herself as a creatress, then by all means she can try to create! But the bottom line is that the female does not have the power to create, any more than the male has the power to conceive.

The female has a womb to conceive, and not a penis with which to impregnate. Medical science can today change the body, but it cannot change the one polarity of awareness into the other. So although medical science can change a woman's body into that of a man, it cannot give her the ability to access the power of the void, or to impregnate, or to create.

You may argue and say, "Yes, that is true, but a woman can go out and create her own business, or she can create a piece of art, or she can create a new type of car, or she can create a piece of music, or she can create anything she wishes to create!" And I say, "Yes! That she can. But is it true creation?"

How many women do you know of who can honestly create something that was never there before? I know of none. Yet there are many women who have nurtured what men have created, and in that nurturing have made it grow into something bigger and better, just as a mother nurtures her children into productive young adults. But it was not the mother who created the children. The mother conceived and gave birth to the children, and then nurtured them into adults. Likewise, women have not created the practice of business, or art, or cars, or music. Whenever women are involved on the creative side of life, it is to conceive and bring to birth the creations of men.

The female can only sustain and nurture that which the male has brought forth with his creative powers. Therefore, when a female starts a business of her own, she is in fact not creating anything new, she is merely nurturing a practice that already exists. Similarly, even if the female composes a new piece of music, she will not be creating music, she will only be using existing forms of composition to bring to birth a new piece of music. Yet those forms were not created by females, but by males.

Look at life in terms of it being a game. Call the game chess. Now remember that relative to the spirit of man, we are all female, irrespective of gender. But it is not us, as females, who created life, but the spirit of man. All we can do is to play the game of life. So we move the chess pieces here, and then there, and so we bring to birth many new opportunities that did not exist at the outset of the game. But can we honestly say we are creating? All we are doing is merely pushing around pieces on a chess board, and although, through that, we are indeed bringing to birth much within the process of life, realise that to bring to birth is not exactly creation.

Yet, the male does create, for he is totally unlike the female. Why? Simply because the female will instinctively nurture the game and its rules. This she does because it is her nature to conceive, to bring to birth, and then to nurture. But the male, on the other hand, will instinctively try to understand the game. In doing so he will tamper with the rules, change them, modify them, alter them, until finally he has destroyed the original game. This he does so as to evolve awareness through the process of learning, something which is as natural for him as it is to hunt and to kill so that he and his family may eat and be sustained within the process of life.

Therefore, on the one hand, we have the nurturing of the female which tends towards preservation, and on the other, we have the destruction of the male which tends towards evolution. Without the male's drive to hunt and kill, he and his family would starve to death, just as without the male's drive towards destruction, the evolution of awareness would become preserved, become frozen in time, and would therefore grind to a halt and die. Yet, equally, without the female's ability to conceive, there would be no family to feed in the first place, just as without her ability to nurture and to preserve, there would be no life left to enhance the evolution of awareness. So once again we see the dual polarity of awareness at work, and how vitally important is the act of intelligent co-operation between them.

Destruction versus preservation, male versus female. However, destruction is very much the act of creation, as paradoxical as this might appear to be, for it is simply not possible to create something out of nothing. In order to create anything we need building blocks of sorts, and the material for that must come from somewhere. This is not a concept I wish to expand upon in depth in this book, for I could write volumes on just this one concept. Therefore let it suffice to say that if we are going to create, we must first tear from out of the fabric of life itself the material with which to create something new. The implications of this are quite clear, namely, that in order to create we must destroy something else. An obvious example of this is the act of procreation.

When a man impregnates a woman, he has not simply ejaculated sperm, as so many ignorant fools are prone to believe.

The mere ejaculation of sperm is a perfectly harmless excretion of bodily fluid, but this is not the same as the act of impregnation which occurs as a result of that ejaculation. The moment a man has impregnated a woman, he has, through the medium of his sperm, ripped out of his own electromagnetic being a small portion of his life-essence. It is that portion of his life-essence which forms the one polarity of a nucleus that will become a new life. However, that one half of the nucleus within the woman's ovum now acts as a magnetic force that rips its opposite polarity away from the female's electromagnetic being, for both polarities are needed for conception to take place. Therefore it is not only his own electromagnetic being which the male has damaged, but also that of the female. But quite apart from this damage to both himself and the woman, the male has, in addition, also destroyed her virginity, and has thereby started up a whole new metabolic structure within her body. Never again will that female's body be the same as before the impregnation.

Nevertheless, realise too that there is destruction and then there is destruction. There is the type of wanton destruction that does not support either life or the evolution of awareness, and then there is the type of destruction that upholds life, uplifts it, and aids in the evolution of awareness, as for example, in the act of procreation. But even here, we need to take care, for just as the act of procreation can be abused in terms of rape, plunder and indiscriminate breeding, so too can we turn any good act into something which is foul and wantonly destructive.

In this respect, we need to remember that whilst the male does indeed produce and ejaculate the life-giving sperm, he also produces and spews forth the germ of all forms. The female, on the other hand, provides the egg and, by receiving the male's sperm inside of her, the egg becomes impregnated, after which her womb nurtures and finally brings to birth the new form that was created during that act of intelligent co-operation between her and the male.

Conception and childbirth are therefore very much the responsibility of the male, just as it is his responsibility to see to it that only those forms which are beneficial to the evolution of awareness are created. However, as is only too clear, men today shun that responsibility, because they refuse to acknowledge that the act of creation is their responsibility. Nowhere is this clearer to see than in that cruel form created by men, and termed sexual promiscuity.

By not taking responsibility for the creative act of procreation, men have pushed that responsibility, their responsibility, onto the woman. As a result, men feel that they are at liberty to sow their wild oats around indiscriminately and even to rape, for in their minds the female body is there for their fun, for their gratification, and for the fulfilment of their sexual lust. Yet, in their efforts not to be constantly pregnant and not to give birth to every Tom, Dick and Harry's offspring, women have inadvertently co-operated with men in the creation of that cruel form. By assuming responsibility which is not theirs, women now mostly take the infamous pill, and thereby keep their bodies in a state of perpetual false pregnancy!

Sad and ironic, is it not? In trying to be incorporated into the world of the male, and in taking the lead of men who are nothing but spoilt and highly irresponsible little boys, women the world over have had to sacrifice their self-respect by learning to live a lie. In trying to be accepted within the world of the boys, and in trying to please and to gratify men, these women are playing the role that has been mapped out for them, and have even convinced themselves that they are happy to have their bodies abused. If the man has set the example that his wild oats are for all and sundry, then why should the woman not spread her legs for every dickhead that comes along and wants to climb on top?

However, the reality is that this is all a lie – a terrible lie, breeding more and more confusion every day. Yet, it seems that confusion *is* the name of the game! "Here, just swallow this pill. It will confuse the natural functions of your body, just as men have confused your mind! But at least in that confusion your body will not conceive, for it thinks it is already pregnant, and in that blurry haze of confusion between one sexual partner and another, you will also not have to conceive the purpose of any of these jerks!"

But in spite of all the confusion, in spite of the woman's denial of her own self-respect, she still finds herself conceiving and nurturing a purpose which is rapidly beginning to destroy everything that has always been held sacred within the act of procreation. Yet this abuse of the sexual act is no different to the abuse men are inflicting upon everything else in the world.

War, famine, illness, unhappiness, and poverty, are all the results, or the manifestations, of man's sense of greed, just as his insatiable greed for sex has brought forth broken relationships, venereal disease, AIDS, and prostitutes. By submitting to their greed, instead of taking responsibility for their creative powers, men have plundered the planet's natural resources in exactly the same way as they have forced their sexual lust upon women. Even in this day and age, and in more than just a few cultures, are women still forced into giving birth to one child after another, whether their wombs can handle it or not, whilst they are made to work like slaves, and are often beaten up for not having pleased the man in some way. Likewise, men still cut down whole forests, and then wonder why it no longer rains, and destroy vast tracks of land with indiscriminate farming practices, and then wonder why the soil is becoming infertile. But, if forests are there for men to plunder, why not females too? If the land is there for men to rape, then why not rape females too?

Oh! I know! There are today certain moves towards nature conservation, just as there are certain moves towards the protection of females' rights. But who is going to protect the planet and nature from a self-destruction that has been created by men? And who is going to protect the female from a self-destruction also created by men? If it no longer rains when and where it should, and if the ozone layer is breaking up, who are the men that will change this? And if females today are only too happy to have a hysterectomy just so that they do not have to endure the messy business of menstruation, and to be sterilized so that they can enjoy sex freely without having to swallow a pill, then who are the men that will change this?

At the end of the day any creation is a sexual act, no matter whether it is an invention, a musical composition, or a baby. But even though creation is the male's responsibility, we must also not forget that no man can create without the female's ovum and her womb. Accordingly, and as we have already noted, it is the male's responsibility not only to contain the female, but also to provide her with the correct lead, for only in this way can she support and nurture the correct values in life.

Therefore, if the rights of women are to be protected and restored in the true sense of the word, and if the rights of that greater female we term the planet are also to be protected, then it is time for men the world over to start growing up fast, and to stop playing around like so many spoilt little boys taking revenge on mother.

If you want to start taking responsibility as a male, the questions you should be asking yourself are, "Do I show the female in my life the respect I should have for the mirror of my own inner female? Do I treat the female with the same respect I should be showing to the world around me? Do I hunt only so that I may feed my family, or do I hunt just for the fun of killing? Do I share with my wife my purpose, or do I only share with her my sexual lust?"

Also, look, and see for yourself, whether you are really taking responsibility for the sexual act. By this I am not just referring to the physical act, but to all of your creative acts. Know that the true male does not share only his physical sperm with the female – he shares with her all of his creative essence at all levels of their relationship, physical, emotional and mental. Realise that it is simply not possible for any female to exercise intelligent co-operation with a man who does not share his emotions, his feelings, his thoughts, ideas, fears, doubts, hopes, desires, wishes, dreams and, in short, his everything. If he remains a closed book and only wants to share in the physical act of sex, it is impossible for the female to conceive his purpose at any level other than the physical act of procreation.

Men who are closed do not incorporate the female into their lives. Their attitude is simply one of wanting to use the female as some sort of glorified servant who also has to satisfy his sexual needs. But just as servants do not share in the life of the master, so too are they not expected to conceive his purpose or his child. For such men the female's only real purpose is to clean up after them, and that includes seeing to it that she does not conceive and bring to birth anything they may in a moment of abandonment have shared with her, irrespective of whether it is an idea, a dream, a fear, or their sperm. Such men expect the female to accept their seed, but not to conceive, in keeping with their role as servants. Even at the physical level, these men are quite happy to leave contraception to the female. But realise that if the female is having to contracept your sperm, she will more than likely also be contracepting your creative essence at all other levels within your relationship.

To understand all of this fully, remember that as the male you carry and secrete the life-giving sperm at all levels, physical, emotional and mental. So, whenever you engage in any form of activity, you are in effect creating something. If it is the action of physical sex you are engaged in, you will impregnate the female, and a child will be the result of that activity. If it is your emotions you are sharing with the female, then once again you will be impregnating her at that level. In other words, when you share your emotions, either quietly, or whilst upset, with the female, she will bring to birth what she has conceived from you. Consequently, if the emotion you are putting out, or your "seed," is positive, then so to will be the outcome of what you have shared, but if your emotions are negative, the outcome will be negative.

Exactly the same is true of thoughts. Realise that if the female becomes negative or pessimistic, you cannot blame her for it, for she is only bringing to birth what she has conceived from you! If, on the other hand, the female "delivers" a response that is contrary to what you have tried to implant in her, then clearly she has contracepted your seed! If this is the case, you need to take a good look at why she is contracepting your seed.

The reason I am hammering this point home is because, as I have already warned, men constantly forget that all of awareness is relative. However, we cannot afford to make the mistake of thinking only in terms of women. As a result of the relative factor of awareness, it happens all the time that men are "impregnated" by another male at either the emotional, feeling or mental levels. Needless to say, it is not really possible for one man to impregnate another, but in practice we all too often see men *behaving* as if they are overly-pregnant! In fact, the effects of such a conception can frequently become very real. This is especially true in the work-place, where employees are always feminine in relation to their boss. But let us look at an example to make this clear.

Andrew works for a man who is given to indulging in all sorts of negative emotions and thought patterns. Andrew is a very conscientious employee who tries his level best to please his boss, and since he does not have too much belief in himself, he is always in female mode whenever he is with his boss. Now realise that whatever Andrew's boss says to him is going to affect Andrew to the very core of his being. If his boss tells him to jump, Andrew does not ask how high, he just jumps as high as he can! But because his boss is a negative man, all Andrew ever "conceives" from him is negativity. So when his boss tells him he is terrible at his job, Andrew sinks into the depths of despondency. When his boss tells him the company is going under, Andrew believes him and becomes morose with worry. When his boss tells him that there will be no Christmas bonus this year, Andrew immediately assumes it is because he is not serving the company well enough. In fact, to put it crudely, the boss is "fucking with Andrew's mind" and, to all intents and purposes, Andrew keeps conceiving his boss's negativity, and in the process believes it to be his own!

Therefore another question you should be asking yourself is, "What have I inadvertently conceived from other men in my life?" If you want to be honest, you do not need to look any further than your social conditioning. How many of your ideas and beliefs are honestly born from your own "seed?" What monsters have you given "birth" to in your mind, in your feelings, and in your emotions – monsters that you conceived from others? In this respect think also of your own mother, and of all the females who have played mother to you, for the mother too is masculine relative to the little boy. What have you conceived from all these mothers?

Finally, take good stock about how you really feel about yourself. Do you feel weak and impotent? Do you feel powerless? If so, why? Is it perhaps because you are allowing everyone around you to "screw" you? If this is the case, then know that it is only because you are not claiming your power as a male, and are therefore throwing everything and everyone around you out of balance. Furthermore, if you are not claiming your power as a male, then it means you are in female mode relative to the world around you, and, as a result, of course every Tom, Dick and Harry that comes along will try to screw you!

In all of this realise that, because of the relative factor of awareness, it is really quite easy to screw a man. However, know also that no-one can screw the true male. A great many foolish men have learned through bitter experience that a hulking male body, a hairy chest and a huge penis, have not prevented them from getting screwed! Physical endowments are great stuff, provided you have the masculinity to match those symbols of manhood! But in order to have that masculinity all of us have to work hard at claiming our power as males. We are born with the physical bodies of men, yes! But we have to unfold our full masculine potential in order to make ourselves into true males.

The true male is a man who is not a willing partner, and accordingly, he can never be seduced. The true male knows his purpose in life, and therefore provides the lead, points out the direction, and prescribes the method to be employed. In addition, by taking full responsibility for the creative act, the true male will always be the one to initiate the act of intelligent co-operation between himself and the female, and will thereby cause her to bring to birth only those forms which he knows for a fact will enhance his purpose, and therefore also uplift all of life around him.

The male acts in this way, irrespective of which female he happens to be with, for even in his relationship with other men who are female relative to him, the true male will acknowledge their own maleness, and will therefore never "take advantage" of them. Instead, he will take the lead in the sense of setting the example of what it is to be a true male, and will thereby encourage these males to claim their own power as males. Also, being a true male, he will, by following his own purpose, point out the direction to these men and, in so doing, will enable them to focus upon their own purpose. Likewise, in prescribing the method to be employed, the true male will take care not to violate the masculinity of another man. Prescribing the method means unfolding our masculine potential, but this does not mean that we must screw other men in order to feel more male ourselves.

The true male treats that greater female, namely, the world around him, with exactly the same respect. Never does he rape her. Never does he plunder her. Always does he co-operate with her intelligently, and, as a result, always does he sow into her the seed of those forms which aid him in claiming his power as a male.

It is said that many a true word is spoken in jest, and nowhere is this clearer to see than in that vulgar expression men so often use, namely, "it's fucked up," meaning that it has been abused to the point of uselessness. The only problem is that people rarely, if ever, pay attention to the truths which they utter. Are you willing to be honest? If you are, then ask yourself these few questions: "What is my world like? Is it flourishing and prosperous? Is my wife happy and contained? Are my children growing up into happy and responsible young adults? What about my work? Is my business flourishing? And what about me? Is all well in my life, or is everything a fuck-up?"

Whether your life is simply less than you would like it to be, or whether it is a complete fuck-up, I am sure that you will be able to recall some stage in your life when you have been told, or else have told someone else, to "stop fucking around." Remember that admonishment now. The male, being the representative of the spirit, initiates every act, and every act is an act of creation, for better or for worse. The impotent, or the infertile man, on the other hand, cannot in fact act – he can only react, that is, re-enact his folly! But to re-enact one's folly means to reproduce one's folly over and over again, and reproduction is a far cry from creation. Therefore we either act and draw upon the creative power of the void like true males, or we fuck around like arseholes reproducing the "abortions" of other jerks! The choice is ours!

So, are men sexual studs? The true male is a highly virile being, yes! Being thoroughly creative from the tips of his toes to the top of his head, the true male is indeed also a stud. However, since he cannot be seduced, he alone will decide when, where, and with which female he will initiate the act of intelligent cooperation. But men who have never claimed their power as males are infertile and, being infertile, they are usually "milked" without scruple by all and sundry, for the seed extracted from them can at best be used only for reproduction! By whatever standards one wishes to measure this concept, I do not think that one can term an infertile man a stud. And any man who allows himself to be "milked" for reproduction purposes, can hardly be termed creative. Such a man is nothing more than a donor of physical sperm.

However, notwithstanding any of the above, I would like to clarify a point that is all too often taken at face value, causing men an undue amount of confusion. The point in question concerns the fact that it is the male who initiates the act, and that the true male cannot be seduced, because he is not a willing partner.

By taking this concept at face value, men often believe it means that their wives must not initiate any act, and that they, as men, should not be open to the suggestions of other men. Yet, if we consider everything we have learned so far, and most especially about how important it is for the male to be open to the female and to the world around him, it is immediately apparent how silly such a notion is.

In the first place, if you are being a true male, you will naturally be incorporating the female into your space and into your world. That inclusiveness will be perceived as a warmth radiating from you, as indeed it is. What's more, since all of life responds positively to warmth, both females as well as males will be attracted to you. In the case of your wife, she will feel drawn to you in such a manner that she will feel the need to return that warmth, but, being female, the only way she can do this is to express to you her desire to support you by conceiving and nurturing your purpose.

At a physical level this means that your wife will often be the one to cuddle up to you, either for a hug, meaning that she wants to be held and included in your world even more, or else in bed, for the purposes of making herself available for sexual intercourse.

Therefore although it may appear as if the female is initiating the sexual act in this case, realise that it is only because you have initiated the intelligent co-operation between her and you that she is now turned on! In other words, your wife is turned on just because you are being a true male in taking the lead in every possible way.

Exactly the same is true at the emotional and mental levels. Because you are being a true male, your wife will want to share in your emotions as well as your thoughts. So if you happen to be deeply preoccupied, she will often remind you that she is there for you by expressing to you her own emotions, feelings or thoughts. Yet by doing so your wife is not trying to assume the male role, she is merely letting you know that she is waiting for you to embrace her into your world.

The same principle operates with other men. Feeling attracted by the warmth of the true male, men also want to reciprocate that warmth, but, being males themselves, the only way they can do this, is by offering you something of themselves. However, that something will, of course, be their own creative power and, as a result, such men will become happily engaged in enthusiastically trying to create some-thing which will serve your purpose. These men are in effect offering you the only thing they have to offer, namely their creative power, not in an attempt to "screw" you, but as a gesture of their willingness to create according to the lead you are giving, and in line with the direction you have indicated.

From all of the above it should also be clear that any sexual problems a man may experience, are entirely due to his own ineptness in the art of intelligent co-operation. To put this in a nutshell, if your wife finds sex with you a bore, it is because you are not being male enough to turn her on. If, on the other hand, it is you who find your wife sexually boring, this is once again because you are not male enough to be turned on by the female, or alternatively, because, by wanting to be a little boy, rather than a real male, you have become bored with having sex with mother!

Nonetheless, I must in all fairness also point out that many married couples today experience problems in their sex life. A substantial number of these problems originate, not from the fact that the man is weak, but rather from the man not wanting to give the impression that he is in any way forcing his will upon his wife. Such a man tries so hard to be a good, kind, loving and considerate husband, that he ends up being so much of a gentleman that he fails to be a hot-blooded lover!

In the majority of these cases sexual problems will arise sooner or later, simply because the female does not feel contained and safe with the male. By not wanting to violate his wife's freedom, the husband who is the "perfect gentleman" will inadvertently fail to "claim" his wife, and as a result will not contain her. But in not being claimed, and in not being contained, the female is receiving from the male, what is for her, a highly confusing message. Such a female does not know how to interpret the lead her husband is giving her. Does she belong to him, or not? Is she really part of his life, or not? Does he honestly want her in his life, or does he only want to use her occasionally for his sexual needs?

As paradoxical as it may sound, every female needs to know that she has been "claimed" by her husband, and that she is therefore the one and only woman with whom he wishes to share his life, his everything. But, having been claimed, she also needs proof upon the physical plane that she does belong to him, not like an old piece of baggage that gets carted around with him, but as his "other half," whom he loves and cares for like himself. In this respect every true female wants or, more precisely, *expects,* to be "taken" sexually by the male! By this I am not advocating rape! I am referring to the fact that it is the male who has to initiate the act, and that it is the male who has to incorporate the female into his life, his world and his being.

The true male cannot ever become bored with the unknown, and in mapping out that unknown, every female is for him an exciting mirror of his own inner female. This is especially the case with the woman he has chosen to share with him his everything, including the sexual act. Likewise is every female deeply inspired to conceive and to bring to birth the purpose of the true male, for within her heart of hearts she knows that it is only by being incorporated into the life, the world, and the purpose of the male, that her own fate can unfold according to the dictates of the spirit of man. As a result, the female feels utterly fulfilled whenever the male "takes" her physically, emotionally and mentally, for in doing so he is making it clear to her that she is one with him, and that he needs her as much she needs him.

To grasp this fully, it may help to think of it in this way. If you want to pick up something with your right hand, you simply do it! So are you imposing your will upon your right arm and right hand? Similarly, if you choose to masturbate, are you sexually harassing yourself? Yet, if I ask you to pick something up for me, and you agree to do so, then you are a consenting adult who has agreed to do something for me. On the other hand, should I order you to do something, and you do not want to comply, but still I force you into doing it, I will indeed be guilty of rape, even if it is not sexual.

The point to be understood here, is that where there is a full commitment between the male and the female and, more specifically, between husband and wife, the female is as much a part of the male as his own body. Consequently the true male will never stand accused of raping his wife, for the simple reason that his wife is his right arm, his right hand, and in short, his every-thing! This does not imply that the female has no rights of her own. It simply means that the true female has no wish other than to be "taken" fully and unequivocally into the life, the world, and the being of the male, so that she may conceive, bring to birth, and nurture his purpose. This the female yearns for, not because she is a doormat, but because she knows that the male carries the life-giving sperm, and so holds within his being the creative power that she needs in order to bring to birth her own fate within this lifetime.

PART THREE

GETTING TO KNOW YOURSELF AS A MALE

CHAPTER FIFTEEN

ROLE MODELS

*That which is learned at the knee of our
parents creates a lasting impression.*

IN THE PRECEDING CHAPTERS we attempted to gain an understanding of the implications of what it is to be male, and why it is that so many men fail to bring out their full potential as males. However, now that you have at least some clarity, you are half-way there. Once we can see what it is we are doing wrong, we can start to change our ways, our behaviour and our approach, and once we do that, we are well on our way to success.

We have already touched upon the all-important concept of self-discipline – remember that everything we have looked at so far can only really be achieved through exercising self-discipline. Therefore we should now look at this concept in greater depth.

Self-discipline is acquired mainly in two principal ways. First, we learn basic discipline from our mothers, in the form of what may be termed the basic values in life. And secondly, we learn discrimination from our fathers. By "discrimination" I am referring to the ability to take out of life what is useful and beneficial or, in other words, the ability to choose between that which is constructive and that which is destructive.

Although we can learn to become disciplined at any point in our lives, it is by far the best to learn this when we are still small children, because, generally speaking, it is only what we have learned as a young child that tends to stick and to become second nature. It is, of course, exactly for this reason that the habits of a lifetime are so very difficult to eradicate, for if you have never learned self-discipline, then it is really rather difficult to learn it later on in life.

As we have already noted, the people we learn from most are our parents, and it is not so much what they tell us, but rather what they show us through example. All children will normally base their behaviour patterns upon those of their parents, because they have taken them as role models. In using our parents as role models there are three major factors that come into play. Firstly, respect for mother; secondly, hero worship of father; and thirdly, the warmth and nurturing we receive from both of our parents. Let us look at these three factors more closely.

It is always at the knee of the mother that the young child learns the basic values of life. These values are inevitably in the nature of respect – respect for food, respect for clothing, respect for money, for animals, for friends, for a home, for cleanliness, for discipline in general and, in short, respect for life. The basic values a child learns from its mother obviously depend very much upon the respect its mother has for all around her, and also upon the child's respect for its mother. Here it is important to remember that the word "respect" means to "look again," meaning that the world is not what it appears to be, and therefore that we cannot afford to take things at face value, or for granted.

The father plays a very different role in the life of a child, for invariably Dad is out working most of the day, and so, when he is at home, he is looked upon as being the loving provider who is also the big, strong, brave defender. As a result, any child tends to hero worship its father, and the really exciting part of the day is when Dad comes home. Furthermore, Dad always seems to have an answer for anything that happened during the day, and since he is the one who normally sorts out all disputes in a way which everyone can live with, he is also looked upon as being the wise one in the family. It is therefore mainly from the father that children learn discrimination, provided of course, that he is a true male. We are not here referring to the guy who arrives home at ten o'clock at night, drunk out of his mind and then beats up his wife before raping her. We're talking about the average male who is trying his best to be a husband and a father.

Even if mother is a doormat and father is a drunk, as children we still learn everything we need to learn by using them as role models, irrespective of whether they are positive or negative models. In this respect it does not matter if we learn how to do something, or if we learn how not to do something.

Either way we learn, and therefore we always have the right parents, whatever we may think of them. However, for the sake of simplicity we are going to look at only the average parents.

A most important point to bear in mind, is that the discrimination we learn from father does, of course, always pivot around the basic values we learn from mother. This is so very important because, in learning how to cope with life in general, the male can only meet the demands of life through his ability to discriminate in terms of what has value or not. In fact, all that self-discipline really boils down to, is the male's knowledge of basic values, and his skill at being able to discriminate between many different values.

However, in order to learn these two aspects of self-discipline, it is also vital that the child grows up in a home in which he receives ample warmth and nurturing. If the child does not grow up with this love, he will not respect either of his parents. In such a case the child will still use his parents as role models, but instead of using them in a positive sense, he will use them as role models in the negative sense. This means that the child will grow up acting out what he feels his parents are doing to him.

CHAPTER SIXTEEN

THE OVER-DOMINANT MOTHER

IN LOOKING AT our parents we should be careful not to take them at face value. For example, over-dominant women fall mainly into two categories. In the first category we have the proverbial battle-axe who makes no bones about the fact that she is the boss, and in the second category we find women who often appear to be meek and mild, but who actually have backbones of steel. Being meek and mild is only a behaviour which allows them to manipulate everyone around them, but if you scratch a little beneath that outer facade, you will find a woman who is every bit as hard as nails. This is not to say that all women who are meek and mild are over-dominant. Some of these women will be genuine doormats who are just too weak to stand up and fight for their rights. In such cases, the driving force behind these women is usually a severe self-hatred, causing them to believe that they deserve no better.

Now, the boy who grows up with an over-dominant mother will usually end up manifesting three very distinct forms of behaviour. Firstly, he lacks confidence; secondly, he tends towards manipulation and laziness; and thirdly, he suffers from a sense of suppressed creativity. Let us look at each of these three forms of behaviour more closely.

The man who lacks confidence has no real belief in himself. Although this lack of belief in self will not stop such men from excelling in the workplace, it is always sad to see how they put all the value on what they have to offer. For these men it is always a matter of, "Do not look at me as a person, look at the excellent product I am offering you." "I may not be a hero, but I am an excellent lawyer." "I may not look like much, but I am an excellent lover in bed." "I may not be a very good husband or father, but because I bring in lots of money, my family lacks for nothing."

Such a man never sees himself as part of the equation, for it never occurs to him that he has value in himself. Seeing his value only in terms of what he can offer as a product, the man tends to focus on delivering those products at the cost of everything else. Therefore if, for example, that product is money, so that his family's material needs are well catered for, then the man will concentrate on working even harder, so that he can make even more money. As a result, he becomes stuck in his routines, most especially the routine of work-make-money. The fact that his family wants to spend time with him, not because he is a walking cheque book, but just because they love him, does not enter his mind.

Lacking in confidence, this man is also quick to become defensive. Always fearing that perhaps what he has to offer is not good enough, he finds it difficult to handle criticism of any kind, even positive criticism. So if you tell such a man that there is another way in which to look at something, he immediately becomes defensive, and if you try to pay him a compliment, he will brush it off as being irrelevant.

Being far too scared to look beyond all the things that are already working for him, even if they are marginal, this man focuses so fiercely on his own little world, that he is normally very rigid in his thinking. Consequently, he is also not at all adventurous, for his motto is, "Half a loaf is better than no bread at all."

Furthermore, through not believing in his own value, this man will often hide behind the female's skirts, not necessarily because he is weak or a coward, but simply because he feels he has no right to ask anything for himself. Therefore if, for example, his car comes back from the garage not having been properly serviced, he will not hesitate to send his wife to the garage to complain. The rationale here being that his wife has value, but not him, and therefore the garage will listen to her but not to him. Alternatively, he will go back to the garage himself, but instead of fighting for his own rights, he will more than likely tell the garage that his wife is not happy with the job!

The second behaviour pattern mentioned above, namely manipulation and laziness, is very much a spin-off from the first characteristic. Having no belief in self, this man also does not believe that he has the power to make a difference in the world around him. Consequently, everything is always someone else's fault, and through not being able to see his own value, he finds it hard to see his responsibility in what is taking place in his life. Always believing that he is at the mercy of everyone and everything, not necessarily because he feels like a victim, but simply because he believes he has no real value, this man is for ever passing the buck in one way or another. So if a project fails, it is never his fault, but yours. On the other hand, if the project is a success, then once again it is thanks to your expertise and skill that it worked!

Yet, this self-effacing behaviour cuts both ways, for by never being able to give himself honest credit, this man also indulges in all sorts of negative feelings about himself. For example, he will often behave as if he is totally inadequate, in the sense of, "I can't do this." Or he will suddenly become highly insecure, in the sense of, "I don't know what to do." And if all else has failed, he will resort to his trump card, namely, "I don't understand what is expected from me, and so how can I act?" All in all, such a man will more often than not try to manipulate others into doing for him what he does not believe he is capable of doing for himself and, in the process, of course, tends to come across as being just too lazy to do it himself!

The third characteristic, namely suppressed creativity, tends to manifest mainly as a lack of imagination in the face of a highly developed sense of logic. Having no flair for adventure, and fearing change, this man likes to have all his ducks in a nice neat row all the time! Also, since he always has to find his value by measuring his own performance against that of others, this man finds it exceedingly difficult to break out of what is considered normal by average standards. If he did, how would he know if he compared favourably or not? So, from his perspective, it is far safer to conform to the norm, which also means that practicality does not form part of his life's experience, for this man believes that in order to excel you must do it like it has always been done, whether it is all that practical or not! As a result, he finds it hard to laugh from the belly. For this man, the folly of life is serious stuff! So what is there to laugh about?

In what we have looked at in this chapter, I have, for the sake of simplicity, painted only the worst case scenario. Obviously every individual is different, and therefore no two people will manifest their behaviour in the same way, nor will they have the same approach towards life. Also, bear in mind that although I have listed all of the behaviour patterns that emerge as a result of having had an over-dominant mother, mothers too are unique and individual. Accordingly, your mother will not necessarily display all of these traits, and since you are different to your mother, you may also not necessarily have all of the characteristics listed here. Nevertheless, the potential for these traits will always be there, and even if they are not obvious now, they may well become manifested at some later stage in life.

What's more, none of us like to show our negative traits. Consequently, we have all learned to mask these characteristics so that they appear normal and therefore acceptable, or alternatively, we have masked them in such a way that they appear to be something completely different to what they really are. Yet, if you are prepared to be honest with yourself, you will be able to see the true nature of all your characteristics.

I have chosen to put the accent on the over-dominant mother, for this is what the majority of women are, since most men in the world today, as in the past, are still very much little boys. Nonetheless, we must also briefly consider the mother who is genuinely weak and a doormat, and the resulting influence this type of behaviour has upon her sons.

The man who has grown up with a doormat for a mother is not difficult to spot. This man is usually a dark, sombre presence, brooding quietly in a corner. Never eager to place himself in the spotlight, and therefore always appearing to be secretive, he radiates an intense dislike for men in general, and if engaged in conversation by either sex, will display an open aggression that is heavily marked by a sarcastic sense of humour bordering on cynicism. The eyes of such a man are filled with unmasked mistrust, or else they have about them a sense of emptiness, along the lines of the lights are on, but no-one is home!

Always feeling victimised and somehow persecuted, this man resents attention when he gets it, and fumes with an unvoiced frustration when he does not get it. Being an utter paradox even unto himself, in that he longs for attention and yet abhors it, this man is for ever at odds with himself and with everybody and everything in his life. Never satisfied with anything, he is also never sure what exactly it is he is wanting or looking for. As a result, he drifts aimlessly through life, or alternatively confines himself to a miserable life of self-inflicted hardship in the hope that he will be able to impress upon the world how hard-done-by he is.

But the sad thing about this man's behaviour is that no-one enjoys being faced by such a mirror of self-punishment, and so everyone tries to avoid him as much as possible. Naturally, this only confirms for this man his belief that he is unloved and unlovable.

Having an almost non-existent self-image, such a man spends his life feeling very sorry for himself. For him life is never a bright adventure of hope, but is instead a total bitch, and every man is a son of a bitch who does not deserve to be treated with courtesy, much less respected!

CHAPTER SEVENTEEN

THE WEAK FATHER

THE WEAK FATHER is a man who does not believe in his own maleness, and who therefore finds life much easier when he hides behind his wife's skirts, often looking deep into the bottle, and talking up a storm! Being weak, such a man has very little intention of standing up for himself, simply because such a bold action is much too threatening for him. Yet, care must be taken not to assume that if you had a dominant mother, you will automatically have a weak father. Being genuinely weak is a far cry from pretending to be weak – something which most men love to indulge in – for in this way they too can manipulate everyone around them. I need to make this point here because, although the world has always been, and still is riddled with weak men, very few of these men are genuinely weak. If pushed far enough, a real bull suddenly emerges! Nevertheless, irrespective of whether the man really is weak, or whether he just pretends to be weak, the effects upon his sons are the same.

The boy who grows up with a weak father, or a father who pretends to be weak, will end up manifesting once again three distinct forms of behaviour. These are characterised by, firstly, a sense of being disillusioned by life; secondly, a sense of being disappointed in general; and thirdly, a suppressed sexuality.

The sense of disillusionment manifests primarily in terms of general apathy, often in the sense of being "helpless" and "powerless." So, this man will look at what is happening around him, and even to him, but will then simply shrug his shoulders and say, "What's the point in trying to change it? I can't change the world, so why try?" But by indulging in the attitude of "Nothing I do is going to change anything," he is also very prone to procrastination, for if his action is not going to make a difference, then what is the rush?

Furthermore, such men also tend to lack any real sense of self-respect, in that any old thing will do. Therefore dirty underwear and socks, an unmade bed, empty beer bottles lying around next to the garbage bin, ashtrays overflowing with cigarette butts, foul language and fast foods, are all quite acceptable. Having no real self-respect, these men also lack honour, and so are not all that troubled about lying, helping themselves to other people's property, or simply "borrowing" something without requesting consent! Yet they are themselves always quick to complain about not being respected, or not being acknowledged, and in trying to get the recognition they demand from others, they are usually extremely adept at scheming and manipulating, although they are not always entirely conscious of the implications of their plots and their manipulations.

The sense of being disappointed tends to manifest mainly as being evasive and cautious. This is very much a case of "once bitten twice shy." Being careful not to expose themselves to possible emotional hurt, these men are normally quite insensitive and, as a result, they unconsciously demand the stiff upper lip from both themselves and those around them, irrespective of gender.

Having a closed heart, these men also lack any real sense of commitment, but like to cover for this by being loud and macho, in the sense of, "Don't worry about me! I'm okay by myself!" Growing out of this macho act is also the characteristic of, "Leave me alone! I want some peace. So why don't you just go away!" But when such men are drawn into conversation, they will, in their eagerness to be acknowledged, often resort to a rather coarse sense of humour, laughing loudly at the expense of others, and especially at someone else's misfortune!

The third characteristic, namely, suppressed sexuality, is always most easily noticed as a distinct lack of creativity. This can range from always having sex in the same position, to always going for a drive on Sunday afternoon! The novelty factor never enters this man's mind and, if it does, he views it as being suspect, or else just too much effort to put into practice. To compensate for his lack of creativity, such a man is often very drawn to some form of aggressive sport, such as rugby, boxing or wrestling. The more macho the sport is, the more masculine he feels, and the energy spent on the sport alleviates at least some of the inner frustration he feels as a result of not being creative.

The man who suffers from a sense of suppressed sexuality is normally also quite obsessed with sex, even to the point of being promiscuous, and often being more than just a little interested in pornography and sexual perversions. Not feeling at all creative, he can only really express himself in terms of the sexual act, even though most of the time he is so eager to please, or to show off, that he is a pretty lousy lover! Furthermore, although he knows deep down inside that he needs to release his suppressed creativity, and not realising that it is his own masculinity he needs to get in touch with, this man can very easily mistake this inner urge for a sexual interest in other men. Such a misinterpretation can manifest in all sorts of ways, ranging from overt experimentation with homosexuality, through bisexuality, to the typical "closet queen" type of behaviour.

There is little point in us considering the influences of the strong father, simply because if you had had a strong father, he would have been a true male, in which case your mother would also have been a true female, and you would not now be feeling the need to read this book. Yet, remember what was mentioned in the previous chapter, that no two men, and therefore no two fathers, are the same. Every individual is unique, and so too is his behaviour. What's more, every boy will have his own particular reaction to his father's behaviour. In this way, even brothers from the same family, and with exactly the same father and mother, can and do grow up as very different individuals exhibiting different character traits. Just remember that the characteristics we are looking at represent potentials that are common to all, and that those potentials can be manifested at any time in life, and under a great many guises.

CHAPTER EIGHTEEN

HUNTING FOR POWER

Now that you have a better perspective on who and what you are, in terms of your behaviour patterns, we can look at how you as a male should be relating to the world around you.

The way in which evolution has set it up is that the male is the hunter. But what does this really mean? Put quite simply, it means the acquisition of knowledge gained through personal experience, and as we have already noted, such knowledge is in reality power – power which we can use in fulfilling our fate, and also in the acquisition of even more power. But, for the sake of clarity, let us see what this means in practical terms.

In hunting for power, the male involves himself in five areas of endeavour, with a two-fold purpose in mind. This purpose is first, to strive for the acquisition of power through the medium of his own private inner world; and second, to strive to achieve freedom by using that power within the outer world, beyond the confines of his home and personal relationships.

When he hunts for power within his inner world, the male gains knowledge in five cardinal areas of endeavour. These are sobriety, action, feeling, warmth and intent. Sobriety is the ability to assess every situation in one's life precisely as to its true value. It is often called clarity, and it is a vital quality, since we cannot take action in our lives without being clear on our circumstances and values. Naturally, such an ability implies having to be ruthless in the sense of standing detached from emotion, and not allowing personal feelings to cloud the issue at hand. Sobriety does not mean having to be heartless, but rather that we have to be honest and objective, even if the truth does hurt! From this, we can see that sobriety is a quality of awareness that is very much based upon knowledge which is certain, and in this respect it is worth noting that the only worthwhile changes are those we make with sobriety.

Action speaks for itself, but it is good to bear in mind that by action we are referring to the implementation of the type of decision which propels us forward in our search for happiness and fulfilment of purpose. It is the action that brings about meaningful change in our lives that is important, and not action in the gym, or action in cleaning the house, or action on the dance floor. Needless to say, true action is a far cry from reaction, and therefore simply to keep on re-enacting our folly is to be caught in what is effectively non-action.

Feeling, as we know, is gut feel, or intuition. This is the

ability to participate in all of life freely without the restraints imposed by logical assumption. Because of their nature, feelings can only be corroborated through later experience. In working with feeling we are working with the heart, and this is the only way in which we can "feel our way around in the darkness of the unknown."

Warmth is the nurturing aspect of the human being. This act supplies the care that is needed by any living thing for it to grow, to flourish and to prosper.

Intent is the ability to place and to maintain the focus on what is most important to you in your life, irrespective of whether this is to nurture a new seedling in your garden, to nurture the dream of having your own home, or to nurture the belief that you are going to succeed in claiming your power as a true male. In other words, whilst nurturing pertains very much to the physical care of someone or something, including yourself, intent means that you keep your focus on what you want, and because of that, you do everything within your power to materialise that wish.

By using the power he has gained from hunting within his inner world, the male also hunts for power in the outer world by once again involving himself in five areas of activity, namely, education, politics, medicine, religion and science. Each of these five areas of endeavour leads to knowledge both within and of the greater whole, and only a little thought is needed to see how knowledge in these five areas leads to freedom. However, so as to avoid falling prey to preconceived ideas and taking these pursuits at face value, let us look at each in turn.

Before we do so, we need to know that one factor underlies everything. The import of this is that if we are to hunt for power successfully, either within our inner world, or in the world out there, we must come to see and uphold the interrelationship of life. There is only one life, and we are all interdependent and interactive units of that one life. Life is just one huge system of relationships. Therefore, our well-being, happiness and success, are entirely dependent upon our skill in relating firstly, to ourselves; and secondly, to the world around us.

However, because people have become so separative in their thinking and in their approach to life, they no longer relate to themselves or others in any meaningful way, and so it is no wonder that people are today so powerless, and that the world is in such a mess. Unless I can relate to a computer in a knowledgeable way, I cannot utilise it. If I cannot relate to you in business, I will not be able to do business with you. If you cannot relate to your wife, your marriage will fail. And if I cannot relate to my right arm, it means that the nervous system in my arm has been damaged, and I am unable to use that arm. Life is exactly the same, and the "nervous system" that enables us to engage life is our knowledge of relationships. Without a knowledge of relationships, we are paralysed and powerless, and will never achieve any kind of freedom.

It is easy to see how education leads to freedom, because unless we have an education, we can never really be free in the sense of being our own boss. However, it is important that education is not seen only in terms of academic schooling. Academic schooling is indeed part of being educated, but true education means that we have the acquired ability to handle life and the many challenges it brings us. The only way for us to acquire that type of education is to make sure that we use all of our "lessons" within life wisely, in the sense of constantly taking stock of our lives with re-spect, for without this education we will end up being beggars, and beggars can't be choosers.

Politics more or less speaks for itself, since it is centred around the ability to negotiate for strategies that allow for the manipulation of power. In other words, we find out what we would like, and then we see how best to interact with others in achieving our goal. This can be as simple as asking several builders to quote for the paving you want to do around your house, and letting each of them know that you are shopping around for the best builder. Or it can be a subtle as telling the school principal that you would love to give the school a donation towards its new sportsfield, but unless the mathematics teacher can give your son some extra attention in mathematics, you are going to have to spend the extra money in sending him to a private teacher. Alternatively it can be as complicated as having to support a nature conservation campaign, in order to win the favour of a local community, whose support you need for a new housing development. Yet the bottom line in all these types of endeavour is politics, leading to the freedom that enables one to materialise one's own wishes.

Medicine implies the freedom from disease, in the broadest

sense of a dis-ease that is caused by an imbalance of sorts. So, in this context, medicine also includes the male's concern with relationships, irrespective of the type of relationship. For example, if his child is struggling with maths, he looks at the relationship between his son and the teacher, as well as at his own relationship with his son and with his son's school. Likewise, if the builders are all too expensive, the male is forced to look at his relationship with the building industry. But in both cases the male will be looking at these relationships in terms of how best to overcome the dis-ease.

Religion is not at all what it appears to be at face value. The true meaning of religion has nothing at all to do with man's sense of separativeness based upon prejudice. So, by religion, I am referring to the human being's innate drive towards understanding him– or herself in relation to the meaning and purpose of life. It is therefore very much to do with building an awareness of ourselves in relation to life, for this is the true meaning of religion, namely, "relating back to the self." In practical terms this amounts to ridding ourselves of our social conditioning, and thus achieving our freedom.

Science very much speaks for itself, since the sole purpose of science is to enhance the quality of all of life, by uncovering information that everyone can use to achieve freedom through the medium of technology, irrespective of whether this is medical technology, mechanical technology, educational technology, or food technology.

Having seen the two-fold approach of the male in hunting for power, let us now take a look at how it actually works in practice, especially the concept of hunting for power in the world at large.

Say that Sean comes to realise that there is a lack of sobriety within his life. The moment he comes to this realisation, Sean will immediately turn within, to start searching for possible solutions or answers to what could be wrong. By going within, Sean will start to look at his behaviour to see what is causing the confusion and lack of clarity. In this particular case, he will of course be hunting for power entirely within the scope of his own inner world.

If, on the other hand, Sean's wife, Mary, senses that their son is experiencing a lack of clarity in his mathematics, she will share this concern with Sean, and now both of them will have to turn their attention to the outer world. Obviously their endeavour here is going to be centred around education, but if they want to find the sobriety they need in order to help their son, they will have to start by questioning whether the educational system their child is following is actually fulfilling its purpose. If they feel that it is not doing so, then both Sean and Mary have first of all to turn within, to start looking at what they feel is wrong with the system, and how best to solve their son's problem.

From these examples we can see that whether the male is hunting for power within or without, both he and the female always have to resort back to their feelings, and therefore to their own inner world. This is, of course, the very meaning of mapping out the unknown. However, after this initial turning within, the male's approach becomes quite different to that of the female, and it is the failure to understand and to make allowances for this essential difference that is so often the cause of violent disagreements between the sexes.

The true female's approach is to use her endeavours in the outer world solely to relate to those inner aspects of herself which she would otherwise not encounter. So the female, in tending the hearth, is forever focussed upon her inner world, even when she is interacting with the outer world. The male, on the other hand, being the hunter, is the one who has to hunt for power in the outer world. As a result, all of his hunting within is geared towards helping him to be a better hunter in the outer world, and this is where the difference lies, for the female, of course, is using all of her hunting in the outer world to help her become a better hunter within.

Looking at our example of Sean and Mary, we can see that once Mary has found the sobriety she needs, and has identified the cause of the problem her son is having with mathematics, she will share her insight with Sean, but will then leave it over to him to handle the challenge. It is not Mary's responsibility to go out and tackle the school principal on the issue of education. Instead, she will present her husband with everything she has uncovered, and will then stand back, in the sense of allowing him as the male to decide what action he will take. And this is as it should be, for it is entirely the male's responsibility to deal with the world at large, and since he is well-equipped for this, Mary must leave him to sort out the problem from there on, if she is not going to start wearing the pants by assuming the role of the hunter.

To get a better handle on this, let us rework the same example from a slightly different angle. Say that Sean expresses his concern to Mary about their son's marks at school. In his attempt to get to the bottom of the issue, Sean will initiate an intelligent co-operation between himself and Mary. He will do this by using his own feelings, coupled with her knowledge of what is happening on the home front. So Sean will start by asking Mary for her feelings on the problem, and will also ask questions about Johnny. Are Johnny's marks suddenly much lower than they have always been on average? Are all of Johnny's marks equally low? Is Johnny always doing his homework, and, if so, how conscientiously? Is Johnny complaining about his schoolwork? And so on. But in all of his questioning Sean will be using Mary's knowledge of what is happening on the home front so that both of them can achieve clarity concerning their son's school marks.

Now if they have exhausted all of these possibilities, and Mary feels that the problem does not originate with Johnny, she will express this opinion to Sean, and then they will start looking in the outer world for the answer. So if, having spoken to their son, they find that the problem lies at the school, Mary, as the female, will turn back into her own inner world to search there for possible answers to the problem. Again, once she has come up with something definite, she will share her findings with Sean. He, on the other hand, being the male, will immediately set out to the school in search of answers, and will start by speaking either to Johnny's teachers, or to the school principal.

In relation to all of this, there is another difference between the male and the female that needs to be noted if we wish to avoid more misunderstandings. This difference concerns the different ways in which males and females express themselves, and it amounts to the fact that even when the female has been able to identify a specific problem, she will often not be able to pinpoint it exactly, not because she is stupid or incapable, but simply because the true female relies much more on gut feeling than on rationality to find the sobriety she is seeking. Therefore it will not be strange for Mary just to tell Sean that she believes the problem lies in how Johnny is being educated at school, or that she feels Johnny is not very happy with his teacher, or that she feels he is perhaps not communicating well with his teacher. From the female's point of view, she knows that she has a very real feeling for what the problem is, but will most of the time not be able to be more explicit than that.

Consequently the female will often just give the male all sorts of feelings, and will then leave it to him to ascertain what those feelings translate into in practical terms. This is especially true if the issue concerns the outer world, as in the example we have just looked at. So, if Mary simply feels that Johnny is not doing his homework properly, she does not need to stop and think it through. Without even having to think about it, Mary will follow her feelings in sorting out both Johnny and his problems with respect to his schoolwork, since this is very much her inner domain and world.

However, if the problem lies outside of her domain, Mary will just give Sean her feelings, and will leave it to him to think out the best practical method of handling the education of his son in the world out there. This point is very important for the male, since men all too often feel that if the female knows that something needs to be done, then she should act upon her knowledge. Yet, although the true female will take action if she needs to, she will only do so within the confines of the hearth and her world. The outside world is very much the hunting ground of the male, and she will leave him to tend to that area, as indeed she should, for if she doesn't, she will be assuming the male role and will thereby be disempowering the male, as well as doing herself injustice.

CHAPTER NINETEEN

THE MALE PERSPECTIVE ON RELATIONSHIPS

IF WE ARE TO PRACTISE the concepts we looked at in the previous chapter correctly, then it is vital that we understand what they really mean. In this respect we have already noted that all of life is a system of relationships. However, in order to recognise these relationships for what they are, and to grasp how to work with them, let us examine what this implies in greater depth.

If we look again at the five areas of endeavour, we see that within his own private inner world, the male hunts for power in terms of sobriety, action, feeling, warmth and intent, all of which are aspects of power. In considering these five aspects it is important to remember that power is knowledge gained through experience, and that all experience arises from action. Bear in mind, though, that even refraining from action is still an action that will yield experience and therefore knowledge. Furthermore, since it is the male who initiates the act, irrespective of what that action is, hunting for power, from the male perspective, is very much in the nature of calling forth experience through the medium of action or, for that matter, non-action.

Accordingly, the way in which the male hunts for sobriety, or clarity, is to initiate the act of conversation. But do not take this at face value. The real reason for engaging someone in conversation is to be able to listen, in order to learn, rather than jabbering away like an idiot, or talking up a storm just because you want to be heard. You cannot possibly achieve clarity on any issue if you jabber away nonsensically, or if you always want to prove your point and be right. What's more, the true male listens as much to what has not been said, as he does to the words that have been spoken. In other words, there is always a very good reason why people will try to avoid talking about a certain issue, and why they will become uncomfortable when the male remains silent. So sobriety has everything to do with the art of listening, and in this respect, initiating conversation can be as obvious as selective speech, or as subtle as not saying anything in order to elicit information.

Action for the male is centred primarily around his duty as the provider. Yet once again this should not be taken at face value. Although the male does provide food or money, remember that he also provides the lead, the direction, and the method to be employed. Therefore, here again we see how important it is for the male to learn to act rather than react, for all of his action must be based upon his ability to discriminate between that which is life-supporting and that which is not. His every decision and move must be geared towards enhancing the quality of life, and supporting the evolution of awareness.

Feeling is the art of entering the unknown. By learning to listen to his gut feel, the male, like the female, listens to his heart in order to use the irrational knowledge called forth through his interaction with the unknown. Remember that the unknown is exactly that, the unknown, and therefore in facing anything which is unknown, the mind is useless. The only way we can handle the unknown, is to feel our way in the dark by using the gut or the intuition. However, because the female will always take the male lead, one way or another, it is vitally important for the male to initiate the act of opening the heart. If he does not do so, but instead puts the focus on the mind, the female, in taking his lead, will also listen less and less to her heart in an effort to become ever more rational and logical.

Warmth is the art of nurturing, which, from the male perspective, is the act of initiating dating and marriage. This is a concept which has become so distorted through time, that it is today very badly understood, if at all! The real implication here is that nurturing, for the male, is his ability to draw upon his knowledge of intelligent co-operation for the purposes of fertilisation. To grasp this fully, realise that we cannot nurture something we do not have. If it is a garden we wish to nurture, we must first have that garden. If it is a child we wish to nurture, we must first have that child. If it is a hope we wish to nurture, we must first have that hope. And if it is your purpose you wish to nurture, you must first know what that purpose is. But for the male to have a garden, means that he must plant the necessary seeds. To have a child means that he needs to impregnate his wife. To have hope means that he must impregnate his inner female with the seed of hope. And to know his purpose, he must "fertilise" the world around him through the process of intelligent co-operation, so that his purpose can be brought to birth, that is, made clear.

Because the male does not have a womb, he can only bring something into existence through the process of intelligent co-operation, or, in other words, through the fertilisation of the female, irrespective of whether this is his wife, his inner female, that greater female: the world, the soil in his garden or his business. But clearly, just as the male has to nurture the seeds he has planted if he wishes them to grow and to flourish, so too must he nurture his family, his business, his hope, his dreams and, in short, his sense of purpose.

Therefore nurturing for the male does not stop at fertilisation, but is rather an ongoing commitment to his endeavours, to his purpose, to his life, and ultimately to the world and to life in general. Consequently, when the true male makes the decision to nurture something or someone, he commits himself, not just to the purposes of fertilisation, but for life. Clearly, this is a huge responsibility, and since it rests squarely upon his shoulders, it is always the male who initiates the act of dating and marriage. Needless to say, this also should not be taken simply at face value, for as should be clear by now, the true male will date his garden, his hope and his sense of purpose, in the same way as he would date his wife-to-be. Furthermore, once he has committed himself to that garden, that hope, that purpose, and that woman, he is married to each of them for life!

From the above it should not be difficult to see that intent for the male means initiating the sexual act for the purposes of creation. But here it is important to remember that any true act is in reality a sexual act, in that it culminates in creation, whilst anything this is a mere reaction only culminates in reproduction, or more of the same. This principle holds true even when two males are working together, for although one male cannot impregnate another male, they will be able to inspire each other through the process of intelligent co-operation. That inspiration is to "all intents and purposes" a "conception" or, more precisely, the joint arousal of the male's creative urge, so that each will impregnate his own inner female. This is something we saw in the example of the Wright brothers working together towards creating air travel. So when he is co-operating with the female, intent for the male is very much the urge towards the fertilisation of his individual purpose as a creator. But when he is co-operating with another male, intent for him is inspiration in the true sense of the word, that is, initiating the sexual act within the process of life so that to "all the intents and purposes" of the greater whole he be-comes a co-creator by fertilising the womb of the unknown.

If we search a little deeper, we can glimpse a vital truth, which is that intent and masculinity are virtually synonymous forces. Yet, more than this it is not possible for me to say in a book of this nature. In time all will stand clearly revealed, but it is impractical to reveal information that cannot be utilised effectively in the life of the average man. Humanity is still a long, long way away from being able to grasp the true secret of gender, and therefore, concepts such as the hermaphroditic nature of man, the relationship of the void to its fringes, and self-fertilisation, are keys to creation that go far beyond what average humanity can grasp, much less utilise, at this moment in time. Furthermore, since creation and destruction are two sides of the same coin, and taking into consideration humanity's present tendency towards wantonly destructive behaviour, it is necessary to be prudent and to leave these keys unrevealed for now.

So let it suffice to say that in hunting for power within his inner world, the male be-comes the product of his intent. By way of a hint to those who have the eyes to see, this means that by tapping the power of the void, the man be-comes the male. We see a faint reflection of this stupendous secret in the development of the physical body, for as soon as a boy starts to ejaculate, his body begins to change into that of an adult man in three principal ways. Firstly, he starts to develop muscle; secondly, his voice breaks; and thirdly, his testicles drop. The implications inherent in this threefold change are as follows.

Firstly, upon the level of the physical plane, the adolescent boy now develops the strength and the muscle needed for action, that is, the act of hunting. Secondly, his voice is becoming resonant with the earth's vibration, meaning that he can now begin to sound his purpose within the act of creation. Thirdly, creation has become possible only because the creative power of the void is now available to the adolescent boy, meaning that this power has been freed for tapping, in the same way that his testicles, by having dropped, have become "freed" for use and, as a result, have started producing sperm.

With respect to the hint I am giving here, it is also worthwhile to note that the pitch of the male's voice, when it is fully developed through correct breathing and training, is the frequency at which he taps the power of the void, and it is therefore also that pitch which determines the quality of his creations. It should therefore not be at all surprising if I tell you that the secret to both creation and destruction lies in the male's ability to modulate pitch, physically, emotionally and mentally. The vibrational frequency of our physical planet is F major, and therefore when the man be-comes the male, it is because he has learned how to harmonise his individual pitch with that key, and has set his intent upon creation for the purposes of evolution. From that moment on his "sperm" is fertile, and all his actions are modulated to the key of F major, for this is the ultimate form of intelligent co-operation upon our planet.

The hint I have given contains an extremely valuable tool for those with the eyes to see, and especially those in the fields of education and medicine. But although such information is invaluable, you do not need to be in possession of it in order to become a true male. Just as it is instinctive for a duckling to walk into the water and to swim, so too is it instinctive for the man to "walk" into his masculinity and be-come the male, simply by changing his "pitch." What holds men back from doing this, is their view of the world. Therefore, to use an old cliché, "Just drop the pitch, man. Just "drop" it!" Do you get the message? Listen to yourself speaking, and listen to the world around you. You already have all the knowledge you need right now, and you are constantly being given more and more guidance.

When he hunts in the outer world for the power that leads to freedom, the true male looks upon education in its broadest possible sense as being the art of recapitulation. This implies the necessity not only to recall, but also to correlate all of our life's experience into one meaningful whole that we can rightfully term knowledge, or power. In this respect, recapitulation is vital for the acquisition of sobriety, since it essentially constitutes the respect of the male, that is, his ability to re-spect all of his world and his life.

Politics has everything to do with what I like to term the art of stalking, irrespective of whether it is someone else we are stalking, or ourselves. By stalking, I am, of course, referring to manipulation, except that I like to differentiate between plain manipulation and stalking. Plain manipulation is an act which is designed so that only you are going to win, and for your own self-centred purposes, whilst stalking is an act designed so that both you and your opponent can win.

Through stalking you still get to win, but not at the expense of the other person, even though it will often be at the expense of their behaviour. For example, and looking again at our previous examples in politics, if you threaten the builder in some way into giving you a better price for your building operations, you will have manipulated him for your own self-centred gain, and this will not necessarily be to his benefit. But if you stalk the school principal into finding out why Johnny is struggling with his mathematics, which you will have done by dropping the hint about the donation versus a private teacher, the chances are that he will look into the matter. In this case you win, Johnny is likely to win, and the school principal will get his donation! Now you have stalked the school principal so that everyone wins, even the mathematics teacher, for when he is questioned by the principal as to why Johnny is not doing well in his mathematics, the teacher has the opportunity to upgrade his teaching methods.

As an example of what is meant by stalking ourselves, consider the meaning of reacting as opposed to acting. If you find that no matter how hard you try, you always end up playing the little boy, then you clearly need to take a long hard look at your behaviour. If you do this, the chances are that you will soon come to the realisation that the problem lies in the fact that you keep reacting out of habit, instead of acting in such a way that you get the desired results. To stop this pattern you will have to teach yourself to be sufficiently detached to observe every situation as if you were merely a witness. Only in this way will you have the necessary objectivity to see your behaviour patterns, to stop your normal reactions, and to do things differently. This is what is meant by stalking oneself.

2) Medicine from the angle of relationships is the art of erasing personal history. By personal history, I mean the you that you think you are, and that you are constantly holding up for everyone to see. In other words, your personal history is in every possible respect your self-image. But unless you can change that self-image, you are never going to have the freedom to be anything other than your behaviour! And this in turn, will mean that you will never get in touch with the real you behind all of that behaviour which comes about because of your social conditioning. Therefore see medicine in terms of healing yourself by changing your self-image.

3) Religion, as we discussed before, is the art of relating to your true self relative to the world at large. Religion is therefore the very core of all possible relationships, and in this respect it has everything to do with what we may rightfully term the art of dreaming. The dreaming we are referring to here is, of course, the act of nurturing, irrespective of whether this is dreaming about your purpose in life, or whether it is dreaming of Johnny getting a distinction in mathematics. The bottom line in all acts of nurturing is being able to relate to intent, that is, the desired goal, in such a way that fertilisation and creation become possible.

4) Science to the male is the art of intending materialisation, so that the unknown can be brought to birth within the

known, through the process of fertilisation and creation. To grasp this, realise that in order to practise any of the first four arts, it is necessary for the male first of all to be-come his purpose. For example, it is simply not possible to erase your personal history if you still want to hold onto your present self-image. By holding onto your self-image you will not be creating anything new in your life; you will simply keep reproducing the same folly over and over again. Similarly, it is not possible to practise stalking anyone's behaviour, least of all your own, if you insist on believing that you are a victim of your birth and circumstances within life. If you hold onto that belief, you will just be reproducing the same thought patterns and the same behaviour patterns that are keeping you in victim mode. So the bottom line in science is intent, centred around the materialisation of purpose, through the act of creation, and this is therefore also the core of all the qualities of personal power the male is hunting for in the world "out there."

With respect to the above, it may help if we digress for a moment in order to look at the difference between personal power and freedom. Power, as we have already learned, is knowledge gained through experience, and therefore personal power is the knowledge we have gained through our own personal experiences. Freedom, on the other hand, is a complex concept, and not one I can explain quickly or briefly. Therefore let it suffice for the purposes of this book simply to state that freedom is the product of using personal power. But this is not all. Realise that every little bit of freedom acquired also generates more personal power, with the result that the two are like the opposite sides of the same coin, and so they are both fully interactive and interdependent.

If we move on to look at the five endeavours of the male within the outer world, we find that in order for him to be successful in those areas he needs personal power to begin with, for unless he already has a knowledge of what he is hunting, his endeavours will not bring freedom. But that initial personal power can only really be gained through the male's endeavours within his inner private world. Only once the male has acquired sobriety, action, feeling, warmth and intent, will he have sufficient personal power to tackle the world out there in pursuit of freedom, for it is these five qualities of awareness that are termed personal power. Those who intend to study my other books will also find it helpful to bear in mind that these five qualities of awareness are what is known as the five aspects of The One Power, as expressed through the male and the female, or, its two polarities, nagal and tonal, the void and the womb.

Education – recapitulation
Politics – stalking
Medical – erasing personal history
Religion – the art of dreaming
Science – the art of interdim materialization
The male must become his purpose

CHAPTER TWENTY

THE MALE PLEDGE

IN OUR CONSIDERATION of this section of the teachings we first need to look at two extremely important concepts, namely, opening the heart, and anchoring the unknown on the physical plane. Both of these concepts pertain to the irrational, and so the only way in which we can really work with them is to follow our gut feel.

The problem is, of course, that we have all been taught to think, but none of us have been taught how to feel, or how to listen to the heart. As a result, most men's hearts are firmly closed, and the only thing they do know is how to think rationally. However, life is not an intellectual exercise, but a feeling. So in dealing with life itself, rational thinking is no good. Rational thinking is only good when we have to discriminate in the process of finding direction, or when we have to work out the practicalities involved within the process of materialisation. Therefore, in dealing with the unknown, and most especially in dealing with the female, we have to follow our feeling, and since all feeling comes from the heart, it is obvious how very important it is for the male to open his heart, and to learn to listen to it. As we shall discover, listening to the heart is also the first step towards true creation.

The most important thing about learning to open the heart, and listening to it, is to take responsibility for ourselves and for everything in our lives. By responsibility, I mean quite literally "the ability to respond" to life intelligently and wilfully, irrespective of whether this is to someone else, to some challenge, or to ourselves. In the case of the male this means the ability to respond intelligently and wilfully to the purpose of life, which is quite simply, the evolution of awareness.

Remember that the male is in every possible respect the physical plane representative of the spirit, and in this sense the command of the male be-comes the command of the spirit. This does not mean that the male commands and the spirit obeys, but it does mean that the true male is a man who is so at-one with his own life that there is no separation between his little life and that greater life of which he is a unit. In other words, the spirit of man is at-one with the universal spirit of manifestation. Since it is the universal spirit's intent to create in order to evolve awareness, the spirit of man too sets its intent on creation for the purpose of evolving awareness.

Therefore, because the whole purpose of creation is the evolution of awareness, and because the male too has this power, the enormity of this responsibility is clear to see. For example, in setting up a business, or in pursuing a career, the prime motive should not be the making of money, but the evolution of awareness, and not only our own awareness, but also that of those around us. In this respect we can create true to the purpose of the spirit, or we can create monsters of depravity that destroy awareness. However, the implication of this is that whenever we respond to life, we respond to the purpose of life. For the male, this means that whenever he responds to that purpose, his creative power becomes aroused, and since it is not possible to live in the world and not to respond to life, the male is for ever creating according to the impulse of life, for better or for worse! This, of course, is true only if he is a fertile male. Infertile men can only re-act to life, rather than respond to it. As a result, they can at best keep reproducing the creations of others, again, irrespective of whether these are good or bad.

Nevertheless, we must be very clear about what it means to respond. The word "respond" basically means the same as "response," meaning "to pledge again." Yet, realise the enormity of the implications here too, for whenever we respond to the world around us, either in a positive or in a negative manner, we again pledge ourselves to that positivity or negativity. So, if we respond positively, we pledge ourselves to the creation of forms that are life-supporting, but when we respond negatively, we pledge ourselves to the creation of forms that destroy.

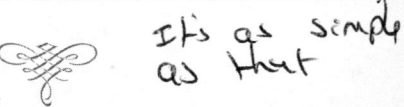

It's as simple as that

In our examination of the implications inherent within creation, we also need to look at the real meaning of reproduction. But, as we consider this concept, it is vital to remember that all of mankind is essentially hermaphroditic, that is, both male and female. With this in mind, we should note that reproduction is the female equivalent of creation. In other words, the male creates, but the female reproduces. However, because every male has an inner female counterpart whose function is reproduction, it becomes immediately apparent how very important it is for the male to remain true to his gender. If he does not do so, he will forfeit his masculine potential as a creator, as a result of having identified with the reproductive function of his inner female. However, notwithstanding the above, remember here that the male is the physical plane representative of the spirit, and that the female is the physical plane representative of the tonal. Accordingly, the evolution of awareness can only proceed unencumbered when there is true intelligent co-operation between the male and the female, between ourselves and our own inner counterpart, and ultimately between the creative power of the male and the reproductive ability of the female.

Always keep in mind that the female, or the tonal, does not create in the true sense of the word, but provides the means whereby the purpose of the spirit can be conceived, nurtured and ultimately reproduced, for only by remembering this can we retain the awareness and the responsibility of what it is to be male. However, this is much in the nature of practice makes perfect, because the only way in which the evolution of awareness can take place, is for the male to try over and over again to create the perfect state of awareness. In doing this, it is absolutely vital for the male to co-operate intelligently with the female, for whilst he is constantly striving to create true to the purpose of the spirit, the female is constantly trying to conceive true to the purpose of the male, which, provided the man is a true male, will be at-one with the purpose of the spirit. In this way they both co-operate intelligently in bringing to birth the purpose of life, that is, the evolution of awareness.

It is this act of the ultimate in intelligent co-operation between male and female that gives rise to what we term procreation. This term is not limited only to procreation at the physical level, since it also includes procreation at emotional and mental levels, for procreation at all three levels is necessary for the evolution of awareness. Physical procreation speaks for itself, for clearly the evolution of awareness would cease if mankind had to stop reproducing itself. But procreation at the emotional and mental levels is also vital, since emotional procreation is the product of the male and the female intending to bring to materialisation their mutual dreams, and mental procreation is the product of them sharing their knowledge in the pursuit of those dreams.

Without this necessary co-operation between the male and the female in the reproduction of their species, the evolution of awareness would cease. And without their mutual co-operation in the reproduction of their dreams and their goals, the evolution of awareness would become a disorderly chaos of disjointed fragments devoid of real meaning because they lack coherency. Consequently, although reproduction is not creation, it is nevertheless just as important as creation, because every creation must be perpetuated, that is, reproduced, if it is to serve its purpose. For example, had the possibility of air travel created by the Wright brothers not been reproduced over and over again, it would never have become perfected, and we would today not have the aircraft that we do have!

Our consideration of the process of reproduction would not be complete without an examination of the vital role of the male in contraception. Realise that it is impossible for the female to conceive anything if the male is practising contraception, or if she herself is forced to contracept his "sperm," physically, emotionally or mentally.

Although we have to consider contraception at all three levels, it is a lot easier to grasp the role of the male if we first look at physical contraception. If contraception is necessary, which it is within any normal marriage, it should always be the male who contracepts. Contraception should never be the female's responsibility, irrespective of what method is being employed. The reason for this is that it is just too confusing for the female to have to contracept.

By this I am not inferring that women are dumb, or that they are incapable of putting two and two together. I am instead referring to the deep inner drives of the female which have absolutely nothing to do with rational thinking, but which have everything to do with feeling and with being a true female. This is most clear to see in the use of the pill, for not only are the woman's bodily functions drastically changed by the constant intake of hormones, but so too is her body kept in a perpetual state of confusion, thanks to the false symptoms of pregnancy. What in effect this boils down to, is that the female is expected to keep accepting the male's sperm, but she is not allowed to conceive anything. In addition, she is constantly "pregnant," but that "pregnancy" never develops, and consequently she can also never give birth to anything!

Yet, realise that men who force this upon the females in their lives, or who encourage the females to take this upon themselves, also treat the female in exactly the same way emotionally and mentally. Such men want to use or, more precisely, abuse the female, and without ever intending to take the responsibility of being the male in that relationship. As a result, these men are every bit as confusing as the pill, and are forever giving the female mixed messages which are utterly confusing. Just as such a man will make love passionately to his wife the one moment, but expect her not to conceive, so too will he embark passionately upon the idea of building a new home, only to tell her the following day that he has changed his mind. Such a man "screws" the female physically, emotionally and mentally, until finally she is so confused that she feels "fucked up." However, realise that, because of the way in which he treats his outer female, such a man does exactly the same to his inner female, with the result that even he feels confused and "fucked up," but by no-one other than himself!

Obviously the easiest and most effective way for the male to exercise contraception, is for him to use a condom. If he does so, then the message to the female is clear, namely, "We are just playing here, and not being serious." Yet, the male must take care that if he does use a condom, he is not also using an emotional and mental condom, which unfortunately is what so often happens. Most men today know only how to share their physical bodies. Therefore, even though they may be excellent lovers in bed, they all too often are totally closed when it comes to having to share their emotions, their feelings, their ideas, thoughts, fears, doubts, insecurities, hopes, wishes, dreams, etc. As a result, these men do not fertilise their females at any level, physically, emotionally or mentally. By not allowing conception to take place, these men then wonder why the female does not support them, and why she cannot bring to birth the wishes and the dreams he has never shared with her!

Therefore it is very much the male's responsibility to prescribe contraception, and how and when he will exercise it. Because it is the male who produces the life-giving sperm, or who contracepts it, it is also he who fertilises the female at an emotional and mental level, or who denies her the opportunity to conceive his emotional stimulus and mental impulses.

If the male takes full responsibility for the act of sex, as well as for the act of contraception, he will always see to it that he does share fully with the female. Knowing that it is his responsibility to show the way and to take the lead, the true male will always make quite clear to the female what is just "the exploration of potential," and what is serious and therefore needs to be conceived and brought to birth. If the male does this, the female is always amenable to exploring one thing after another in their mutual pursuit of fulfilling his purpose, for deep down inside she knows and trusts that when the male has found his direction, and pointed out the goal, he will take the lead, and by fertilising her at all levels, she will also be allowed to conceive that goal, bring it to birth and nurture it into full materialisation. But until then the female is quite content to keep aborting the old in favour of the new, and so even starts to regulate her menstruation. In this respect, it is interesting to note how the true female who is taking the lead of a strong male, will unconsciously start to menstruate at any time of the month, simply because the male has indicated a change in direction!

Before we leave this section, one final word of advice is called for. Contraception practised by the male must not be seen as a license to engage in pre-marital sex. The reason for this is that sex is ultimately the act of creation, and as such it should not be practised other than between husband and wife. If we take into consideration everything we have learned so far, we can see that there is great validity in the old-fashioned practice of courting, during which the male is "shopping around" to find the right female mirror. If the male is good at courting, both he and the female will greatly enjoy the time they spend together. In addition, they will also learn much from each other. But because the male, in order to be a true male, must be fully committed for life, he cannot simply take a woman on approval.

By engaging a woman in pre-marital sex, the man is in effect expecting the woman to allow him to indulge in the pleasures of a marriage that is not a marriage, and a commitment that is not a commitment. But realise that in having seduced a woman into such a co-operation, the man has manipulated her into prostituting herself to the consummation of a non-commitment. Even though many such women can settle down to a good marriage at some later stage in their lives, the fact remains that they are second-hand, because of having been some other man's play-thing, and this is no different to the feelings of abuse experienced by the woman that has been raped.

From the perspective of the true male, it makes no difference if the female consents to this type of manipulation or not. As the male, it is entirely his responsibility to provide the correct lead, and therefore simply to take a woman for his sexual gratification, but with no intention of honouring that act, is not something the true male can justify, even if the woman is begging him to bed her! Although there is hardly a sexually active male on this planet, including me, who has not at some stage in his life been guilty of seduction, none of us can actually justify such an abuse of the female. Initiating the sexual act means taking the female, but in doing so, the male's commitment must be for life! If it is not, he is leading her up the garden path for his own self-centred purposes.

CHAPTER TWENTY-ONE

COMPETITION

COMPETITION PLAYS a very important role in the life of the true male, since to compete means to strive together. Remember that the male is essentially very much at one with the spirit of man. Therefore, the principle of unity is very important to him, whether he is aware of it or not. As a result, the male is a creature who seeks companionship and camaraderie amongst other males. In this respect, unless he has been trained in giving the female due respect, a male will often put his own male friends first and, in doing so, will neglect his own wife.

From what we have noted above, true competition is clearly not what people today think it is. True competition is in fact the camaraderie that exists between males striving to achieve their own full potential. So competition is not a matter of being *better than*, but is instead an attitude of, "If you can do it, then so can I," or alternatively, "Come on! If I can do it, then so can you!" In other words, competition is very much in the nature of mutual support, mutual encouragement, and mutual sharing.

Remember though, that the world is not what it appears to be, and therefore we should not take this concept only at face value. For example, say that your best friend, Tim, has marital problems, in that his wife, Julia, is flirting with other men. What can you do for your friend? The answer is, nothing! Why? Because you are not Tim, his marriage is not your marriage, and his life is not your life. Furthermore, because Tim, like all males, is a representative of the spirit, he must fight his own battles if he is going to believe in himself. Therefore you cannot help Tim as such, for any help you give him will be implying that he is too weak, too incompetent and too incapable of fighting his own battle. This is true of helping any male, for if you do, you only succeed in disempowering him.

Consequently, the only "help" you can offer Tim, is your support. There are many different ways in which we can support someone. You can support Tim by constantly, but surreptitiously, singing his praises to Julia. You can support him by offering him your empathy, but not in the sense of commiserating with him. If you do commiserate with him, you will only encourage him to indulge in self-pity, in which case he is less likely to want to fight for his marriage. By empathy, I mean that you are there for him whenever he needs you, even if it is just to be his sounding board. But by far the greatest support we can give anyone, most especially another male, is the simple expression of heartfelt warmth. A quiet but affectionate greeting, the offer of a drink, quiet time spent together, a ready ear, a genuine sense of humour, in the sense of being able to laugh at the folly of life, and a warm smile, are all truly precious gifts to the male who is having to face the loneliness of fighting a battle no-one can help him with.

Although none of us can fight battles for another male, we can always be there for that male, by supporting, and also by offering our encouragement. By believing in your friend, and by expressing that belief to him, you will encourage Tim to start seeing his own value, and thereby you will encourage him to fight for his rights. Sometimes our challenges in life are such that it can be difficult to see that we do have value and therefore have a right. But unless we can see that we do have value, and because of that, we also have the right to fight, we invariably fall into the trap of wanting to step back and admit failure. In moments such as these, encouragement in the form of, "Fight! You are worth it!" is invaluable. Sometimes the person concerned cannot find anything of value in himself. However, simply because someone in his life wants him to fight, that person will fight like a Trojan, not necessarily because he believes in himself, but because he does not want to disappoint someone who believes in him! This is very much in the nature of, "Even if I am worth nothing, I have nothing to lose in giving this battle my everything, so that at least you can draw some honour from my actions. In this way, I can at least become worthy of your belief in me!" Such is the poignant beauty of the human spirit.

The third thing you can do for your friend, Tim, is to share with him your own experiences and knowledge. Although Tim must find his way by himself, and have his own experiences in order to uncover his own knowledge, it helps every male greatly to know that he is not alone in his struggle to be a male. Sometimes our challenges can appear to be huge, but by being able to compare our challenges with those of others, we inevitably gain a more balanced perspective, a greater sense of competency, and therefore also a greater belief in ourselves and in our capabilities.

It is often said that shared laughter is twice as much fun, and that shared sorrow is half the burden, and so indeed it is! There is nothing more beautiful than two males sharing with each other their joy and their sorrow, for although each knows that he must and will stand alone in his knowledge, within his heart of hearts each also knows that in that sharing he is not truly alone, but instead all-one with his friend, because of the unity of the one life. Standing side by side, each fighting his own battle, two such males cannot possibly be more alone. Yet that is only ever in the sense of being all-one with the one life, and because of that, also all-one with everything and everyone.

However, mutual support, encouragement and sharing, is not, or at least should not be, something that is practised only between two friends. Being the physical plane representative of the one spirit within the one life, the true male upholds this value within all areas of his life. Therefore if Tim happens to be your neighbour whom you hardly know, and you are the man Julia has taken a fancy to, you will not treat the situation any differently. On the contrary, you will use this challenge to win Tim's friendship and trust. Likewise the true male will also look upon his competitors within the business arena, not as men who have to be suppressed or annihilated, but as potential allies, or even friends, competing together to unfold their full potential, and thereby claiming their power as males.

From what we have looked at here, it should be clear that the true male is not a man who feels threatened by the capabilities of other males. Instead, he feels inspired by their accomplishments and so, strives to match other males step for step. Consequently the true male also does not feel the need to "screw" other males, but tries to inspire in them the sense of competition, so that he and they together can push each other to new heights of achievement that would not have been possible without competition. This is what I like to look upon as enticing other males to compete with oneself. The reason for doing this is that the true male thereby inspires in both himself and others a strong sense of having to develop and draw upon hitherto untapped potential, and that potential is, of course, masculinity.

However, think of how horribly wrong this has gone in the world. True to his ignorant ways, man has turned competition into something ugly and destructive, and therefore instead of enticing other males to compete *with* them, to the mutual benefit of all, most men today are far too busy competing *against* each other to notice the destruction, and most especially the destruction to the sense of unity, companionship and camaraderie. Consequently, disharmony, chaos, fear, hatred, doubt, prejudice and suspicion, reign supreme in a world that is becoming ever more disjointed and fragmented, as men become ever more frightened and separative in their thinking.

CHAPTER TWENTY-TWO

THE JOURNEY AHEAD

IN THE TIME YOU and I have spent together through the medium of this little book, I have endeavoured to point you in the right direction. Now it is up to you to take what you have learned here, and to use it in helping you find your way through life as a male. If you do this, you will find that the information you have been given will start to open up new areas of experience for you, and that experience will be new knowledge gained, meaning new power gained.

Take it one step at a time, and I can promise you that it will not take you long before you will start to live that new knowledge. This is what is meant by claiming your power. No-one can do this for you. Only you can claim your power.

As you learn to claim your power, you will begin to learn what it is to be a true male. How much you learn will depend upon how much power you are capable of claiming. If you manage to claim only a little power, you will also gain only a little knowledge of what it is to be male, but if you claim much power, you will learn a great deal about being male.

I cannot tell you how long it will take you, or how much you are going to learn or achieve, for this is entirely up to you. As a representative of the spirit upon the physical plane, you must never forget that there is no manual on the evolution of awareness. Just as the spirit has to write its own manual as it goes along, and just as there is only one life, and one spirit, so too must every man learn to stand alone in his knowledge of self, and learn to write his own manual. However, the biggest responsibility of all, resting squarely upon the shoulders of every male, is that being a representative of the spirit he cannot plead ignorance, he cannot say, "I don't know how." We all come into this life not knowing how. Then slowly but surely it begins to dawn on us, that if we don't find out for ourselves, who else is there to tell us how?

Whenever we are in need of guidance, the only thing we really have to do, is open ourselves up to the world around us. Remember that the world is feminine, and the Great Mother of all is always willing to teach us, to show us the way, provided that we are willing to open our hearts to her and to heed her guidance. Let your vision of the purpose of the spirit be based upon that which our Great Mother teaches us all. In other words, as a male you must cultivate the ability to respond to life sufficiently to draw from it that which you will need upon your quest for maleness.

I have sketched for you a map of the terrain which many of us have already crossed, and if you use this map wisely, it will help you greatly. But realise that as a man you must now plan your own quest, and choose your own direction. Above all else, you must pledge yourself to your sense of purpose. How you do this, and what you understand as being your purpose, is entirely up to you as an individual, provided you bear in mind that, as a representative of the spirit, you are first and foremost a creator, playing your part within the greater purpose of the one life.

Believe in that pledge, and believe in yourself, for at the end of the day, it is all you have. Along the way you will find other males on the same quest, and when you do find these men, walk together for as long as your paths coincide, for in that companionship you will learn much from each other through mutual support, mutual encouragement, and mutual sharing. Remember those males always, and in that remembrance of your mutual quest and camaraderie, do not forget that in moments of loneliness, or in moments of despair, you will find much courage, and draw great strength, from recalling that "to compete is to strive together," and "If you can do it, then so can I!"

ALSO BY THÉUN MARES

UNVEIL THE MYSTERIES OF THE FEMALE
What is true success for a female?

Having proved that they can do almost anything as well as, or better than, men, more and more women are disillusioned with the empty promises of feminism. In their search for success women have been tricked into trading a vital part of themselves for male-like qualities that will never bring them lasting happiness or fulfilment, for, as this book shows, success as a male is no success for a female.

Toltec warrior and seer Théun Mares shows how women can get back in touch with their true feelings concerning their femininity, and how they can reconnect with their innate mystery, to discover their individual purpose in life. He explains the reasons why it takes so much courage, strength and dignity to listen to your heart and to be female. He reveals how you can recapture the excitement, spontaneity and vitality that lead to enduring fulfilment as a true female.

THIS DARNED ELUSIVE HAPPINESS
Théun Mares in this book shows that our most natural instinct is to be happy and fulfilled. What gets in the way is our social conditioning.

Taking us on a journey in which he explores such issues as the underlying differences between males and females, Théun reveals how we can use these to achieve new knowledge, intelligent co-operation and harmony out of conflict. He explains how we can rediscover the essential skills of passage and come to a new understanding of everything we have learned about life, our relationships with other people, our gender, and especially ourselves.

More than anything else at the moment, people are seeking answers to life and relationships. This book presents practical and down-to-earth solutions in response to this growing need. It explains that we cannot handle our relationship issues in isolation. They need to be addressed in the context of how we relate in all areas of our lives.

INSTITUTE FOR THE STUDY OF MAN
Practical courses and workshops.

Elizabeth Schnugh is director and founder of the Institute for the Study of Man, which provides practical courses based on the Toltec approach to life.

Her ten-year experience as financial director of a large multinational company convinced Elizabeth that a radical change was needed in the ways we do things, as well as in the ways in which we relate to each other, and life in general.

She has worked closely with Théun over the past few years to design and present a series of courses with the emphasis on providing people with tools with which to uplift themselves and to change their lives. In addition to her courses for adults, she also runs weekend camps and courses for teenagers.

Elizabeth says: "The bottom line for every single person is to believe that they do have the answers for themselves. We teach people to address the issues in their lives from where they originate, rather than treating the symptoms. What this boils down to is handling relationships, for at the end of the day, all of life is about relationships. We give people practical tools to transform all types of relationships, and we address them at all levels."

For further details, as well as information on organising courses in your country, please contact:

INSTITUTE FOR THE STUDY OF MAN
PO Box 2294, Clareinch 7740, Cape Town, South Africa
Telephone: +27 21 683 5892
Fax: +27 21 683 0084
E-mail: elizabeth@toltec-foundation.org
Website: www.uplift.co.za

THE TOLTEC TEACHINGS SERIES BY THÉUN MARES
This series of books provides a more technical background to the concepts introduced in this book. Toltec means "a man or woman of knowledge," and the Toltec tradition developed as a practical approach

to life, focusing on practical issues that arise in our everyday lives. This is because the only true knowledge is that which we gain from our own lives, out of our own life experience. Gaining our own knowledge implies that we are taking full responsibility for our lives, and since it is not easy to take such full responsibility, this tradition has also become known as the Warrior's Path.

Although the core truths of the Toltec tradition can be found hidden within all true religions, the Warrior's Path is not a religious or spiritual practice. Nevertheless, through developing your awareness, and by learning to see the interconnectedness of all life, you will begin to experience the underlying unity, as well as the essential truths that lie at the heart of all of the great belief systems.

BOOKS:
VOL 1: RETURN OF THE WARRIORS
VOL 2: CRY OF THE EAGLE
VOL 3: THE MISTS OF DRAGON LORE
VOL 4: SHADOWS OF WOLF FIRE (June 2000)

REVIEW COMMENTS:
- *Conscious Living – Australia* – "Without a shadow of a doubt, this book's clarity offers a wide path to intellectual freedom, spiritual joy and utter personal power."
- *Napra ReView – USA* – "This is deep, intense, rewarding material, ultimately leading to the achievement of true freedom and empowerment."

READER COMMENTS:
- "The work is clear, well-written and highly-informative."
- "the path of this philosophy is useful in my daily life and is not escapist in any way."

ORDERING OUR BOOKS:

Order our books from your favourite bookstore.

Alternatively, detailed ordering information, as well as
online purchase options, can be found on our websites:
www.elusivehappiness.com and www.toltec-foundation.org

For direct sales in the USA, call toll-free: 1-888-822-6657

For direct sales in England and neighbouring areas call:
Telephone: +44 1825 723398
Fax: +44 1825 724188

Otherwise please contact us directly.
Lionheart Publishing
Private Bag X5, Constantia 7848, Cape Town, South Africa

Telephone: +27 21 794 4923
Fax: +27 21 794 1487
E-mail: lionheart@toltec-foundation.org
Web: www.toltec-foundation.org and www.elusivehappiness.com

Come and visit our website for interesting articles, new insights
into handling life and relationships, as well as online advice and
sharing of experiences in our discussion forum.